# IN A NEW LIGHT

## A Personal Exploration Of
## The Human Aura

## Mark T. Smith

Copyright 1995

In A New Light

Library of Congress Catalog Card Number: 95-95197
ISBN# 0-9649624-0-3
First Printing, October 1995
10 9 8 7 6 5 4 3 2 1

Additional copies of this publication can be obtained through
mail order by calling (800) 879-4214. Bookcrafters, P.O. Box
370, 615 E. Industrial Drive, Chelsea, MI 48118.

If you would like to contact the author or find out about lecture
schedules and book signings, he can be reached through e-mail
at: aurorasmit@aol.com.

Additional information is featured on the Internet home page for
*In A New Light* at http://www.aurorasmith.com

# DEDICATION

for my father
William Anthony Smith


Requiem aeternam dona ei Domine, et lux perpetua leceat ei.

"Grant him eternal rest O Lord, and let perpetual light shine
upon him."

# ACKNOWLEDGEMENTS

The author wishes to recognize the following people for their love and help over the years, making my life (and this book) possible.

John Fatland, M.D.
Russell Tilley, M.D.
Raymond Moody, M.D.
Rev. C. John McCloskey, III
Rev. Frank Burch, S.J.
Robert Montague
Robert McEachern
Chalmers Wood, II
Constance Abbott
Mary Phillips

# CONTENTS

# FOREWORD

We're all really lucky, it seems to me, to be living in an era in which we have given ourselves permission to re-explore the old spiritual modalities that for so long have been relegated to the dusty back rooms of the mind. What in the world is an aura? How many times over the last twenty years have I been approached by someone who excitedly and cheerfully praises me for the vibrant color and wise deportment of my aura? And I, for my part always proudly accept the compliment, even though I've never had any idea what they were talking about.

Until Now.

Hallelujah! I am pleased that my wonderful friend Mark Smith has put down a great deal of information on this hazy subject. I am especially pleased that he has made his new book into a manual - actual exercises to perform - so that I can finally see for myself.

Mark writes here not from the perspective of some abstractly esoterical theoretical construct, but from his own personal experiences that he has had as he waded out into this most peculiar dimension of the human mind and spirit. And as I know him as a friend, and as a fine and sensitive person, I look forward to retracing his steps through this intriguing new labyrinth.

For the informed on this subject, such as myself, his work - free as it is of incomprehensible verbiage - seems the ideal place to begin. And I suspect that many others will be probing this realm, too, with this guide book in their hands.

RAYMOND A. MOODY, M.D., Ph.D.

# PREFACE

Having grown up in the Kenwood area near Washington, D.C., on a cherry tree lined street that rained pink and white blossoms in the springtime, I was accustomed at a young age to natural beauty and a wonderfully loving, fully functional family. My Montessori school teacher mother, who stayed at home until I finished grade school, encouraged me to be anything I wanted to be. Taking an early interest in both music and science, (wanting a violin for my third birthday, and a chemistry set the following Christmas), my curiosity was broadly based, but cruelly taxing on her nerves. This, coupled with a propensity for knives inserted into light and electrical sockets and a love for all things pyrotechnic, made my minding a full-time job. When I wasn't climbing the bookcase (and pulling it down on top of me), I was releasing the parking brake from cars parked in the neighbors' driveways. I thought nothing of walking into their houses unannounced and turning on their hi-fi's or playing their pianos. No wonder they had a block party the day I started school, making me shake their hands, congratulating me on surviving to the ripe old age of five.

Survival up to that point, however, was by no means assured, nor were the risks limited to self immolation, or neighbors who wanted to kill me. In fact, I almost "checked out" at birth, being six weeks premature and under three pounds in weight. Thought to be hydrocephalic, the doctor didn't give me much chance for survival, especially since the thermostat in the incubator at the Sangley Point Navy Base near Cavite City in the Philippines, was broken and kept trying to fry me. My Navy Commander father, who was stationed there at the time, had some clout and within 48 hours was able to arrange for a seaplane to fly Dr. John Fatland (U.S.N.), with me in his arms, up north to Clark Air Force Base and a properly functioning incubator. Told I probably wouldn't survive the trip, my devoutly religious parents credit Divine intervention (and the U.S. Navy) with my safety and survival.

It was at this time that I had my first out-of-body experience and my only near-death experience. As vivid today as it was when it happened, I found myself floating above my isolet, looking at this red prune-like thing with tubes attached wondering if there wasn't some mistake. This couldn't be the body I was supposed to be in. Something was wrong here, and I didn't like it.

As I was hovering near the ceiling of this room shaped like an "L", I was aware of both hot and cold sensations with heat coming from directly above, the cold emanating lower down around me. I also remember the walls being a purple color, and my isolet was off in the short end of the "L", separate from the other babies down in the long end of the room. The "Voice" that wasn't a voice said I should go back into that body, and that everything would be fine, not to worry. For one of the few times in my life, I was instantly obedient.

Whenever asked what my first memory was, even as a child of 3 or 4 years of age, I referred to this experience. I also remember, from about that time, vivid images of guardian angels, sometimes as many as seven, more often 2 or 3 at a time. Also quite vivid is the memory of telling my mother that "when we die, it's like waking up from a life of dreams". She would look at me with a puzzled but supportive expression and say "...ah...that's right dear." She would also threaten to send me "back to the wild Indians" from whence I must have come.

It wasn't until the fifth grade at 11:30 a.m. on a Thursday morning during a math test on fractions that I had my next out-of-body experience. Once again I was above my body, looking down on my head, floating at the top of the ceiling. And again the entire room was visible in a way that can't be adequately described, but was instantly recognizable as similar to the near-death experience I had as a 48 hour-old infant.

This spontaneous out-of-body experience was not caused by any type of trauma; I had a total of six by the time I was 21, each experience more intense than the previous one. The cumulative effect of these experiences led me to believe I had a "vocation" to the priesthood. Never having heard of out-of-body or cosmic consciousness/astral projection before, I only had the religious culture I was familiar with to try to make sense of these OTHER states of consciousness. I also referred to them as "spiritual orgasms," for lack of a better description, since words are inadequate to fully cover the range of sensations and emotions these experiences evoke. But you *know* when you have one.

After college and a stint as a Jesuit candidate, my life began to come full circle again, as I began touring the country as a professional musician, playing acoustic guitar and singing my own compositions opening for groups like Jefferson Starship, Jeff Beck, and Grateful Dead members Bob Weir and Jerry Garcia's bands. I'd come a long way since my first piano recital at age 4, playing now to 20,000 instead of 20.

I was also lecturing at college campuses across the country on Handwriting Analysis, doing some TV appearances, and teaching people how to see auras.

But it was during a performance in Iowa that my life truly came full circle when I met the Navy doctor who delivered me thirty years prior in the "L" shaped, purple-walled room.

He and his wife Donita, the chief nurse at the old dispensary, had kept in touch over the years with my parents by religiously exchanging Christmas cards ever since our return from the Philippines. That's how my mother alerted them to my concert schedule which included a stop in Des Moines. My father need not have threatened to disown me should I fail to see them while I was there, because I was actually quite excited by the prospect of finally meeting my "birthing" parents.

As I pulled into the long driveway and approached the large colonial home surrounded by acres of rich farmland, I was somewhat apprehensive having never talked to, or even seen a picture of them. But I was overcome with emotion as they came bounding out the front door and down the steps, arms outstretched to enfold me in a welcoming embrace. We all started crying many joyful tears standing together arms wrapped around each other, hugging and kissing.

This amazing moment was eclipsed only by revelations that yes, it was an "L" shaped room, and the walls were painted mauve, with paint left over from the redecoration of the Admiral's quarters. They told me no one was supposed to know about the paint, since it wasn't navy regulation battleship gray; they did it just to "liven up" the place. I was also told that I was put in the corner of the room near the closet, to keep me away from the other infants who might pass on germs.

I found out that Donita was pregnant with fraternal twins when I was born, and she also delivered prematurely, losing the boy. They always felt a special kinship with me, thinking that I was "the one they saved." Dr. Fatland grew serious as he said, "I've done some research on this and can't find a smaller surviving baby on record the year you were born. I don't know why you're here, but you're definitely here for a reason."

So too I think are we all.

# PROLOGUE

I could feel his energy and warmth immediately when he first put his hands near my body - massaging and smoothing my aura, drawing me upward. I was woozy for sometime after that. A lot like being tipsy, or just out of a sauna bath. Very relaxed - but not depleted. In fact, strangely elated, tingly, . . .

I definitely felt the "energy", but it wasn't until one month later when a sigmoidoscopic exam during a routine checkup revealed a polyp in my colon that he told me about at our first session, that my last vestige of skepticism vanished....

# I

## Seeing the Aura

It couldn't possibly happen. There is *no way* you can see an aura! Maybe in your dreams, or on old paintings of the saints, but not here, not now, *not in my living room!*

But that's exactly what I was seeing almost 20 years ago as my friend was standing right in front of me explaining the simple techniques anybody can learn. Even, apparently, skeptics like me. Maybe I didn't see colors, and the shape and intensity was constantly changing, but there was no doubt about it. That bright silvery envelope was 1 to 3 inches around his head and shoulders and it wasn't going away. In fact, the more I looked, the brighter and larger it became!

That's how it all started. That's how I got hooked. Within a few days I could see colors. Then I found out I could see my own aura in the mirror using the same basic technique. I started reading books, mostly old esoteric out-of-print guides on color meditation, explaining what each color meant, and what part of the body each color's vibration affected. It was like a door to a wholly new world had opened up to me. This was a world that was going on all around me, a world the ancients and wise people from every age knew and took for granted.

This was the start of a journey which never ends. As I learned more, I learned how little I knew. And it all started that late summer afternoon as the sun cast a soft even light in my old studio apartment three floors above "N" street just outside Georgetown.

Here's how you too can "see the light":

Stand the subject 18 inches in front of a plain white background. Have them relax and breath deeply. For best viewing, you need to be at least 10 feet away, and the lights should not be too bright or focused directly on the subject. Natural off-set lighting is best. The technique to view the aura requires that you *look past* the head and shoulder area. Focus on the wall behind the figure. As you stare past the outline of the body, you will very quickly notice a fuzzy white or grayish silver "envelope" surrounding the body. It almost looks like a light is behind the person, pointing up.

Then most probably it will disappear.

That's because the natural reaction of most people as they first see this envelope is to inadvertently change their focus to the person, not continuing to stare at the wall. As soon as you go back to focusing on the background, the envelope will reappear. You must train your eye not to revert to normal focus. That's the hardest thing to learn. Once you've mastered maintaining your gaze through the person, you will notice that colors, shapes, rays and even secondary auric fields will be readily visible.

It may take some time. Although I could see the envelope or as some say "Casper the friendly ghost" right away, it took me three days before I saw colors - but what colors! Yellow or pink is first for most people, then blue, green or purple. Some of you lucky ones will see color right away.

A few people I've trained never see any color with the exception of yellow now and then. But everyone has at least seen the envelope. If you wear glasses, taking them off might help, although most students do better to keep them on. The type of light is also a controlling factor. Fluorescent light is the worst, natural indirect light is the best. Direct sunlight is too strong and will overpower and wash out the aura. Candle light is also very good, but be careful not to cast shadows on the viewing background.

Try various subjects. Get them to breath deeply and exhale fully. One hint: have them recite the alphabet slowly, taking breaths after every two letters. Then speed up after the letter "M" finishing all the rest of the letters without taking a breath if possible. You'll see a change in the aura as the breathing pattern changes.

Another helpful hint: have the person rock gently from side-to-side. You will see the aura move with the person. Sometimes it stays right with the subject, while with others it will lag behind. You might see a ball of color over one shoulder, or a strong bright line of light down one arm. These may pulsate then vanish.

There is no right or wrong aura, no one color better than another. Some shades of colors aren't so good, but the brightness and clarity of the aura denotes various stages of wellness, peace and happiness. Clear and bright is better than dull and murky. The charts at the end of the book will illuminate the color spectrum and should be taken as a general guide to understanding the meaning of each color.

Most often, people have a base color, such as yellow that is close to the body, and radiates no more than 1 to 3 inches away from the head and shoulder area. This color may be mixed with another color, usually the next higher or lower color on the spectrum of light.

For example, a yellow base will mix with green or orange and might appear like chartreuse one moment and then revert back to yellow as you continue to stare, then turning once more to orangish pink before stabilizing around yellow.

The human aura is generally not stable, changing according to internal as well as external stimuli. Everything we do, say or think influences our energy field. The color we radiate is affected by our physical surroundings, as well as the people we come in contact with and the energy field they radiate. What we eat and drink, and any medication we take, contribute to our overall picture. Even our breathing pattern changes the aura as you saw in the previous exercise.

We all talk about "vibes" or "chemistry" between people. First impressions are formed in an instant. Much of this is due to visual clues: general attractiveness, facial expression, clothing, physical presence and posture. Whether positive or negative, we consciously analyze and rate other individuals within seconds after we meet. Subconsciously we do the same thing: "vibes," or "chemistry" may be "intangible" but the interaction of energy fields provides us with "gut instincts" that may be more subtle, but just as telling about the ultimate level of compatibility.

This is why we won't like some people who others may be drawn towards, or like someone immediately who might not be the most physically attractive. They just have a certain "something" you can't put your finger on that attracts or repels you. This "something" just might be our electro-magnetic vibration which is visible to us as the "aura" when light passes through it (and "felt" when we become sensitive through training in Bio-Energy Therapy).

The speed of the vibration determines what color we see. "Infra" red which is below the base of the color spectrum is a long, slow wave. Orange, yellow, and green are progressively shorter, faster waves, and easier to see. Blue and "ultra" violet are the fastest and hardest to see, typically showing up in the "outer" aura which is distinct from the brighter "inner" aura we first learn to see. Some people do possess violet in their inner (etheric) aura, and it denotes great spiritual attainment. Seen in the outer (astral) aura it shows great spiritual capability. Likewise, gold is a highly evolved color and shows great power. It might appear as a ball of energy above the head or on top of one shoulder.

At classes I've taught, students have actually seen golden "rays" radiating upward from some subjects, or geometric shapes like triangles around others. Some subjects appear to be wearing dunce caps that extend 2 to 3 feet above their heads. These phenomena are witnessed by up to 60 people at a time, and when asked to write down descriptions of what they saw, a majority would corroborate these images in great detail.

And now you have the basic technique to see the aura! Like any other muscle, you need to "work out" to develop and maintain the strength of this new found ability. Try several different people in several different surroundings keeping in mind the basics: white or neutral color wall, indirect lighting, subject at least 18 inches away from the wall and 10 feet from you. Most importantly, stay focused on the wall, not on your subject.

Now, isn't finding one of your long lost "sixth senses" fun? You can even see your own aura in the mirror. Just throw your focus on the wall or whatever is behind your image, and as you stare (and breathe), you'll see it.

Don't be discouraged if you don't see colors right away. Keep trying but relax. When you do see colors you might gasp or make some kind of exclamation because the colors, although subtle at first, are actually quite intense. With practice, you can begin to see auras in a variety of settings under various lighting conditions and in front of less than optimum backgrounds. With any luck, this new found talent will become "second nature."

# II

## Feeling the Aura

If you remember pictures you've seen of angels, or holy men and women, they invariably are depicted with light surrounding their heads or sometimes their whole bodies. Often "rays of light" are shown emanating from behind the head and shoulders, and these rays extend in a geometrical fashion. This is true in all cultures and religions. Buddha, Mohammed, Vishnu, Moses, the Prophets, the Saints and Jesus Christ are all shown to be enveloped in light, usually golden or silver - clear in color.

Could it be that before we became saturated with all of the modern forms of media, humans were routinely able to see auras? Is it possible that these abilities are suppressed by our reliance on technology and our faith in science? Have we let the conscious rational mind totally discount our subconscious selves? Perhaps a re-discovery of these innate talents will open up a whole new (old) world, and provide an enrichment not found in modern forms of entertainment.

Certainly, my life has been changed with the discovery and use of these skills: first seeing the aura, then feeling it. In fact, my life was probably saved by the use of "Bio-Energy" and the therapeutic techniques involved in healing through the auric field. This actually happened on my first visit to the house of Mietek (pronounced ME' a TEK) Wirkus, a Polish emigre from what was then Communist Poland. It was 1986. Mietek, his wife and daughter had recently come to the United States, and were starting to introduce these techniques in the Washington, D.C. area. They brought with them a wealth of knowledge and experience new to the West, but used extensively throughout the Eastern Bloc and Russia.

Mietek had demonstrated unusual healing gifts as a child and studied at the Kirlian Institute in Leningrad and the Popov Institute in Moscow after which he was assigned to a workers union clinic and sometimes saw more than one hundred patients a day. As incredible as it seems, he is able to help these people without becoming physically exhausted himself. The secret of this tremendous endurance was learned through studies with a Tibetan teacher who taught him the "breath of youth". Once learned, it allows a person to let great amounts of energy channel through them without fatigue or burnout. You will remember how changing the breathing pattern changed the aura you saw, and the effect of proper breathing cannot be over-emphasized for maintaining good health. It's one of the most important factors in transference of energy, and he uses proper breathing in every "treatment."

These Bio-Energy therapy sessions are conducted as a faster (and frequently better) way to treat illnesses such as fever, cramps, muscle spasms and neurological disorders, allowing the surgical physicians to function more effectively in a critical care role. Used in conjunction with standard Western medicine, Bio-Energy therapy was found by the doctors in Poland and the Soviet Union, who incorporated these techniques starting in the early 1980's, to be most beneficial in Pre-and Post-op cases, reducing pain and promoting quicker recovery without the side effects associated with drugs.

When I first met Mietek, I was teaching a class on auras at the Burmese Embassy in Washington, D.C. Each month about sixty people came to learn the simple technique described earlier. It was in this ideal surrounding of a large alabaster ballroom with crystal chandeliers and mirrors, that the techniques for seeing the aura were mastered.

It was at this time that a student came to me with an article about a man who not only saw auras, he healed people without ever touching them. The following month I was surprised to find this man and his family in my class.

He spoke no English, but could understand much of what was said; his multi-lingual wife Margaret, filled in the rest. She told me how happy they were that someone in America was doing this work and they seemed genuinely impressed with the content and form of the lecture I had just given.

Margaret then asked me if I might like to come to their house for dinner where we would discuss the possibility of teaching these visual techniques to their students.

Curiosity was a main factor in my acceptance of their invitation, but I also felt a sense of fate drawing me toward them and their new and strange world. It's as if I knew that I was being called to do something I would have never chosen to do on my own. Something I didn't really want to do. My natural skepticism was going into overdrive, and I certainly didn't have a belief structure based in the occult. But then I would never have believed you could see an aura until it was casually pointed out to me. After all, my middle name really is Thomas.

# III

## First Encounter

It may be difficult to believe that a person who was already teaching a class on how to see auras would be skeptical of Bio-Energy therapy, but I was highly dubious with a definite "show me" attitude. This skepticism remained even after our first meeting, when this course of study was described to me in detail. But I agreed to teach his students whenever needed and just at the end of the evening, almost as a lark, I asked Mietek if he would "do me".

Not knowing anything about the technique, I would be an objective observer, and vowed not to "give in" to whatever lay ahead. I was strong and healthy, and even though I was a little sore from over-exertion at the previous day's softball game, my only complaint was a sore right tonsil.

As he gently motioned to me to stand and step out to the center of the room, I made a silent check of all body parts and found: a sore right elbow from throwing the softball too hard, a sore left knee from sliding into second base in shorts, and the aforementioned right tonsil. I was rather smug in my confidence that none of these mirror ailments would be noticed. I would merely observe the technique, say something nice about how good it felt, thank them for dinner, and go home.

But a strange thing happened. Not only did he stop suddenly and work on each place that hurt, but he also found an area in my lower abdomen which he returned to twice, a place where I felt no pain. He also seemed to spend a lot of time in my heart area.

I could feel his energy and warmth immediately when he first put his hands around my aura - massaging and smoothing it, drawing me upward. I was woozy for some time after that. A lot like being tipsy, or just out of a sauna bath.. ...very tingly. I wasn't sure what had happened, but I felt something, and that couldn't be denied. The feeling of warmth, especially when he lingered over a certain spot was unmistakable. So was the light-headedness and feeling of calm relaxation.

Yes, I could definitely "feel" the energy, but my skepticism remained. Yes, he had discovered my sore spots, but was much more concerned with my heart and stomach, which didn't hurt. After all, what could be wrong with them if I didn't have any pain in either region?

But how to explain all the rest of the experience? I really was needing to sit down for a moment after he finished, and there was this wonderful peaceful feeling. He was accurate about the knee, elbow and tonsil and he was genuinely concerned about my heart. Margaret asked me if I'd had a death in the family recently, or if I was under a lot of stress. "This could be causing my heart congestion," she said.

"Do you drink?"

"A little," I said remembering we drank wine at dinner." Good," she said. "A little red wine, or better yet, cognac can be very good for your heart." I was wondering at this point how much *they* drank.

Actually they seemed very sober, but I had many more questions now than answers, and was ready to explore this phenomenon further. The knowledge that I would soon be meeting with their students made me ever more curious. Maybe they would be able to prove or disprove the validity of what I had just experienced. She went on to say that some people experience cold, or even sharp, brief flashes of pain when the energy touches an area of "dis - ease." At least I felt warmth and was comfortable throughout the session which lasted only about five minutes. Maybe he just read me wrong.

Then another strange thing happened.

Within a week I happened to notice some blood in my stool. I contacted my old family doctor, and he recommended I get a full upper and lower G.I. series along with a rectal exam. It was also necessary to look at my blood. I just hate needles!

"You've got to take the blood test again. The lab must have screwed up," said the doctor, "no way your cholesterol and triglycerides could be so high." Normal readings are under 200 and 100 respectively. Mine were 280 and 660! On the second try, cholesterol was "down" to 250, still considered somewhat worrisome, but triglycerides were up to 780.

"You have liquid fat for blood" he said in his best bedside manner. "The sample is coagulating in the test tube. It's amazing you haven't had coronary failure. Perhaps your quite normal blood pressure was the saving factor, along with the fact you don't smoke."

No wonder Mietek was concerned with my heart!

And then they found the polyp.

During the sigmoidoscopic exam they discovered a small one centimeter growth about 12 inches inside my large intestine, which turned out to be benign. "Could have been there since birth" my M.D. reassured me after it was removed. "It might have taken years to develop into cancer. In any case it's gone now."

Once again I was reminded of that first visit to the Wirkus' house. They had warned me to get a checkup for my heart and stomach little more than a month before, and now I had just been through surgery and placed on a radical fat free diet! It was only then that my last vestige of skepticism about "feeling" the aura vanished.

# IV

## The Teacher Goes To School

I began teaching people how to see auras in Mietek's classes and found I was the only one there who wasn't a health care professional! Physicians, nurses, chiropractic, osteopathic, massage therapists of all denominations, and members of the psychiatric profession were booking his classes months in advance. The reaction of these (mostly) American Medical Association (AMA) style medical professionals was striking in that they seemed to have come about their understanding of these alternate techniques cautiously, over time, but like myself, had overcome their ingrained skepticism through personal experiences and the hard evidence that something was definitely happening.

What started out as curiosity, or in some cases a desire to "de-bunk" the notion that a person's health could be affected by "massaging" the aura, soon became profound excitement with each new discovery of these hidden powers within the human organism: we could both send and receive energy!

But what exactly is this energy that is apparently transferred from one individual to another? John White's book "Future Science" lists more than 100 terms from ancient to modern sources for what he calls the "X-energy."

Although currently unknown to Physics, this energy which is outside the four known forces of electro-magnetism, gravity and the weak and strong nuclear forces, seems to be responsible for psychic/paranormal phenomena, such as Bio-Energy transfer, and the human aura. Research organizations such as the Institute for Noetic Sciences, the International Society for the Study of Energies, and the International Association for New Science are all studying this scientific problem.

Meanwhile, Mietek asks me if I want to study with him. After teaching three of his study groups, I'm becoming fascinated with the whole phenomenon and it's at this point that he admits me, his first non-medical professional. The classes are really taught by his wife, Margaret, since Mietek speaks very little English at this point. He starts each class (limited to 12 students) by scanning each student as we stand in a circle and hold hands. The first thing you notice is his very noisy and deep breathing: The so called "breath of youth". The second thing you notice is the incredible warmth and tingling that goes through the body as he places his hands around your head and shoulders and in front of your chest and stomach, drawing the energy up your spine.

At first, the classes seem too simple: Just relearning how to breath, staring at a candle flame, visualizing your "cave" or safe haven, focusing on an orange dot on the wall. Each exercise is practiced for an entire month before you proceed to the next one. As we progress, we learn to incorporate each exercise with the one preceding it. Breathe, visualize, meditate; that's all we had to do.

Then we pair off and stare at each other's forehead or "third eye" chakra. We stare into a mirror at our own "third eye". Shapes change, faces distort, animals or old people appear. It's quite disconcerting at first, but having a partner to share in the ordeal helps a lot. The face can even vanish if you stare long enough. We learn how to keep our eyes open for several minutes at a time, never once blinking. I wear contact lenses and can still go over 10 minutes without blinking. During that time, my face or the face of my partner takes on a kaleidoscopic panorama of people both younger and older, foreign or even alien, all the while staring just at the forehead.

Then we learn how to feel the "ball of energy" between our hands. Soon after that, we feel the energy field of our partner. We're putting together all these techniques and exercises, and . . . it's working! We can feel, as well as see, the auric field and can raise this energy anytime we want to do it. Experiments with physical objects in or near the auric field shows how quickly and profoundly things like magnets and crystals alter the natural state - and not for the better!

Other elements like bee glue extract and amber actually increase the auric field in color and intensity. These effects can be seen and felt. Suddenly we are no longer skeptical of these energy fields, but wonder when the medical establishment will start to incorporate these techniques. The amazing thing is we have physicians in the class and *they* are saying these things!

In all, the basic classes take six months to complete. We continue to work on breathing and visualization techniques which increase our energy flow. It's almost shocking that at the end of these basic classes, we can see such changes in size and intensity of the aura, and feel this "ball of energy" growing all around us. A few may increase in some ways more than others, but we're all quite a bit more "energetic" than when we started.

After this, if you are selected and wish to continue, the advanced class delves into much greater detail about specific diseases and their treatment.

# V

## A Most Interesting Event

I'm invited to progress to the next level. Mietek says I have a "big third eye" and would be a good candidate to learn the healing techniques. These classes meet once a month and are much more anatomically oriented. We must learn all the internal organs and the various parts of the brain. It reminds me a lot of human biology classes I took in college. Fortunately, I already know most of my physiognomy but this is a good refresher course. We're given charts and diagrams of the body and are taught how to scan the body, head to toe. Mietek, through Margaret, explains about meridians — a concept from the Chinese system of acupuncture — and energy flow to and from the chakras — energy centers in the body, according to yoga. He still starts each class with the circle of students holding hands, as he walks inside "smoothing" our energy fields. During this period of study, we are asked to work with friends and relatives to gain practice and to experience new and different energy fields. We then meet and discuss our experiences.

At the start of one class, after we break the circle and sit down, he (through Margaret) asks if we've run into any interesting cases. I raise my hand and describe a therapy session which had occurred the previous day involving a woman complaining of migraines. Normally by this time in my training, I can always feel some energy around the head of everyone I work with. In this woman's case, even after some basic massage around the neck and shoulders I could feel nothing. Finally after 20 minutes of energy work, I could feel a slight cold tingle, but no warmth. She informed me that her migraines were fairly frequent in recent years and that sometimes they lasted for three or four days before subsiding. This one was severe and was in its 3rd day, and I was a last resort since medicine didn't seem to help. She left claiming some relief, but I knew I hadn't been very effective.

My question to Mietek was, "Do all migraine sufferers have total energy block above the neck?" Mietek became unusually animated and spoke to Margaret very rapidly in Polish. "Mark, how well do you know this girl? Are you romantically involved?" I worked with her in the office and we'd been in a local theatrical production together (as the romantic leads in "Foxfire") but were not personally involved at all.

"Do you know her well enough to ask her some personal questions?"

I was a little puzzled when Margaret asked about what had occurred six years before: a car accident? or a fall? Neck injuries to cranial vertebra C-5, C-6? Then she asked me to find out if she had problems with her left ovary, did she have irregular periods and did the migraines fit into a 60-day cycle of occurrence?

When I saw this woman next, she felt better and I was able to ask her about her medical history, specifically about neck injuries, car accidents, irregular periods, left ovary problems and frequency and pattern of migraine attacks. As she proceeded to answer these questions, I could almost see the gears turning and the light bulb go off over her head. Yes, she did have a car accident six years ago and cranial vertebra number C-6 was damaged, which caused her first migraine. But the migraines went away until three years ago when her left ovary was removed, and yes the migraines started happening about every two months after that! She was excited to discover this link in her pattern of illness and was surprised she hadn't noticed the parallel between periods and migraines before.

I was amazed by the incredible accuracy of diagnoses, specifically cranial vertebra number C-6 neck injury and left ovary problem, and all of this done on a patient Mietek had never seen!

I had to wait another month before I could ask Mietek my next question, "Is this the standard diagnosis for a woman with migraines?" Once again Mietek spoke rapidly in Polish and Margaret said, "Mietek warned you not to take on the energy of the person you are helping. You must learn to block the energy from coming into you at your wrist. You Americans are so open and empathic, Mietek was able to read her illness from you even though you had seen her the day before. In your extra efforts to help her, you left yourself open and did not exercise your meditation and visualization techniques for your own protection."

I'm afraid I don't remember too much from the rest of that class, I was so overwhelmed by this demonstration that all I could say at the end of it was "twenty years from now I'll be able to tell people I studied with the great Mietek Wirkus." Margaret laughed and in her typical humble generosity said, "Twenty years from now people will say they worked with the great Mark Smith." . . . .

# VI

## Jumpstart

Certainly one thing about my life has been "great" since that bout with the sigmoidoscope and surgeon. That is my health. I can see the effects that "the breath of youth" causes not only on the healed, but in the healer. Often I'll be tired, and don't really want to teach class, or to start a therapy session. But in just minutes, with deep breathing and calm visualization, my energy returns. By the end of class, or therapy sessions, my energy is much higher than it was at the start. Sometimes it's hard to go to bed if the session was held late in the evening; I feel so energized and alive. I've even gotten phone calls at 2 or 3 a.m. from people I've just worked on who are themselves so "jazzed up" they can't sleep.

A woman who was in my class learning to see auras, was also coming to see me for Bio-Energy therapy. She was very troubled by what she thought was another "being" who would try to "speak through her" most often when she was meditating. As I started to work on her energy field, she would begin this unintelligible guttural speech and almost seem to float away in a trance. In the first session, I even had to catch her as she began to fall backward.

Talk about not being grounded! But she seemed very

sincere, and possessed a very brilliant purple aura. There was also some chartreuse and gold in the inner field and the colors seemed to be fighting for dominance.

As the classes and sessions progressed, changes were notable. The "voice" was still there, but she didn't try to "float away" and her aura became more stable, settling in on purple and golden colors. But after a session she was so energized she couldn't fall asleep.

However, one man who had trouble sleeping due to cancer, experienced the opposite effect. He was wide awake early one morning when I started the session, lounging on a couch reading the newspaper. He asked if he needed to be standing for the therapy session, and as this was the first time for him, was alert and curious about the impending therapy session. I assured him he could remain on his side needing only to put down the newspaper and remain relaxed. Having just returned home from several days in the hospital, his wife informed me of his inability to fall asleep.

He watched me with a curious smile as I started to smooth his aura around the head. Working my way down his chest, I could really feel the enlarged lymph nodes all over his torso, but especially in the groin area. Within a minute or two at most, he was not only asleep, but snoring loudly! His wife covered him with a blanket, and later told me he slept until noon, when she was forced to wake him to take his next dose of chemotherapy. His cancer went into complete remission soon after that for several months. Although it would be impossible to claim Bio-Energy therapy had anything to do with it, at least he was able to sleep soundly after that one session.

This may be the greatest benefit of these types of non-invasive therapies: to reduce or eliminate certain symptoms or pains without detrimental side effects or the use of drugs, the body is given the chance to heal itself. It's the same as if your car had a low battery and couldn't start until you got a "jump" from another car's fully energized battery.

The energy transfer between human beings appears to be the same. We talk of being "cheered up" by a visit from a good friend, or a letter from a loved one. Taken one step further, this sending of love in close personal proximity, face-to-face, here-and-now using these healing techniques, "super charges" the body's electrical system.

The effects are the same regardless of any belief (or disbelief) system we may adhere to, and these sometimes dramatic benefits have been witnessed in infants and animals, where the "belief" that they will get better (the so called Placebo Effect) can't possibly be present. Whether we "want" to or not, the energy is still present, and received when sent, just like a letter from a lover.

What is just as amazing is the health and well being imparted to the sender. Properly done, this energy transfer happens spontaneously, and is merely directed by the sender, or channeled in a gentle way to the receiver. A strong feeling of love and wanting to help the person should be the motivating factor, not any egotistical idea that "I" did it. The greatest healers will say "I" had nothing to do with it when asked how they achieve their successes. The more open and loving the sender, the more this loving energy is allowed to pass through undiluted, and it enhances both participants in a truly wonderful way.

In the Aura class, when a student's energy is seen to be depleted, or cloudy gray, we conduct a little experiment. As the subject continues to be viewed by the rest of the class, they are told to rub their hands together, and place them in front of their bodies palms facing up. Placing my hands over theirs about 4 to 6 inches above the center of the palm, my hands moving back and forth slowly, they will start to feel heat and some slight tingling sensations. As I am kneeling in front of the person, the aura around their head and shoulder area is still visible to the rest of the class.

Within moments the effects of this "jump start" are readily visible. The aura will grow in size and brightness, often dramatically. Whatever color was present is usually strengthened and often changed to the next higher frequency. Sometimes the aura will be "taken over" and mimic whatever color I'm showing at the time. Even after I move my hands away, the aura will continue to show rejuvenation and once charged, will grow on its own.

You can try it yourself. Once you have practiced seeing the aura enough to spot the "halo" of each person within a few seconds, you're ready to experiment. You can use various substances such as magnets, crystals, watches, necklaces or precious stones and place each item on the top of the head of subject to be viewed.

Start with a baseline or unadulterated scan of the auric field and notice the qualities and characteristics. Even if you can't yet see color, determine the shape and size and luminance of the aura. If color is visible, watch for any changes in hue and intensity as well as clarity and radiance once the object is placed on the "crown" Chakra.

If there is more than one other person present, you might try to write down your findings individually and compare notes afterwards. This also gives you more than one subject to view, and noting the changes between different individuals is a good exercise.

With two other people present, it is also possible to recreate the "jump start" described earlier. Standing face-to-face and sideways from the viewer, each person should lightly rub their own hands together for a few seconds. Placing their hands, palms open but not touching, over/under each other's, subtle changes will occur in each person's aura.

In some cases the aura will appear to be repelled by the other person's aura, almost shrinking away from it; other times the individuals' auras will actually begin to merge or meld together. If both subjects are asked to think about love, or someone that they love, even if it is not the person in front of them, subtle or sometimes dramatic changes occur and are visible immediately. You can try to think of other emotions as well: hate, fear, worry, jealousy, etc. with similar immediate (but different) results.

Now you can "see" in the physical body's external auric field the changes brought about by "mere" thoughts and emotions.

The ability to visualize the aura is one of those doors that some would not want us to open. Previously considered the private reserve of mystics and clairvoyants, this knowledge was considered dangerous for mass consumption and is still burdened with esoteric or possibly even occult overtones in some circles. But then until recently, books on something as benign as handwriting analysis were also grouped in the occult section of the Library of Congress. Now both handwriting analysis and studies of the human aura are listed under the heading of psychology.

This occurred when some pioneering scientific types like Dr. Shaficia Karagulla, M.D. studied clairvoyant manifestation or what she called "Higher Sense Perception" in the mid-1960's. Her book, *Breakthrough to Creativity* described her scientific background and the methodology used to explore the unknown aspects of the human "super-consciousness." Dr. Karagulla investigated and later witnessed the fantastic experiences of true clairvoyants, *some of whom were her fellow physicians*. They regularly diagnosed illnesses by touch or inner insight, as well as by "seeing the energy fields around human beings."

So it is left to science to prove the nature and effects of the human energy field, because with the advent of Kirlian Photography in the 1930's, we can no longer dispute the existence of such a field. Further research is being conducted in this country, and elsewhere, which suggests the importance that these minute electro-magnetic fields have within and surrounding the body. Mainstream science, in places such as the Menniger Institute in Kansas, and the National Institutes of Health in Maryland are actively engaged in the study of these bio-electrical phenomenon, with some surprising results.

Did you know, for example, that the human body has an entire network of (hitherto unknown) microscopic nerve fibers that permeate every organ and tissue type? They are chemically connected to the pineal gland, itself a little known pea sized object at the base of the brain? Or that there is measurable electric current in the blood stream and other tissue not directly related to the nervous system? Until very recently, established medical thinking would not have allowed for the possibility that such things might exist.

These and other recent discoveries suggest that we might not have been as knowledgeable as we thought about the inner workings of the human body. Dr. Harold Moses of Vanderbilt University, the past president of the American Association for Cancer Research recently said, "What we've learned about cancer ...in the last 10 years is incredible, and 80 percent of that knowledge has been gained in the last five years." He thinks major breakthroughs in the prevention and treatment of cancer are within our grasp in the very near future.

# VII

## Heaven On Earth

Just imagine what effects these thoughts and emotions cause in our "internal" physical state!  Recent studies by scientific researchers show a strong correlation between our emotional state, and our immunological system.  The relationship between brain wave activity and pulse rate, body temperature, breath rate, galvanic skin emissions, pupil dilations, gastric flow, and now, immune response is well documented.

Can our emotions and thoughts make us sick?  Do we "think" ourselves into "dis-ease"?  Is there some way our body gets disrupted by negative stress factors, possibly of our own making?  The evidence including the changes you've just seen in the aura emphatically support that notion!

Does that mean you can "think" yourself well?  Do you keep yourself healthy on a day-to-day basis without even knowing it consciously?  Are prayer and meditation good for us on a physical as well as a mental and spiritual plane?  The answer again is emphatically yes!

The power of prayer in the healing process is also well documented.  And what is prayer but a concentrated emotional exercise directed with an open and humble heart to a

Higher Being in order to effect a positive change in self or others? You are in effect requesting a "jump start" on the cosmic level. The energy you send is amplified through divine intercession when you actively hope (and pray) for help.

The popular expression "Be careful what you wish for, it might come true" shows how often we do experience success in attaining physical goals through a mental or emotional outpouring. Physical action helps, but "the wish is father to the thought" is another popular old cliche' which demonstrates our deep seated understanding that some things tangible really do have their origins in the intangible realm of the mind. It isn't hard to see the link then between the mind and the healing process. The mind and the body are one closed and inter-linked system and each cannot be separated from the other.

Modern medicine however tends toward specialization of skills and compartmentalization of treatment. Anyone who has had a recent experience in a hospital knows this frustrating truth. Each separate department will want its own samples of blood, urine, etc., even though you just gave samples to another department not half an hour previous. Medical "techniques" may be wonderful for treating specific symptoms, but where is the healing "art" needed to maintain the health of the whole person? Yes we can accomplish miracles with modern medicine, but often in a dehumanizing way, with side effects almost as bad as the illness itself. Treatment of the whole system, body and mind, is ultimately the path we must follow.

This combination of new scientific techniques and "old" healing arts is in fact happening as the medical community gives grudging acknowledgment and acceptance to many "folkloric" natural remedies, previously disdainfully dismissed as "superstitions." Science is proving, for example, that certain foods and natural herbs offer a wide range of medicinal benefits, some curative, others preventive in nature.

The debate over the effects of electromagnetism on the human organism, however it turns out, at least raises the question of whether the use of these "good" technologies like the television, computer, cellular phone, or even proximity to electric power lines can have a "down side" of increased incidence of illness including various cancers. Our health as human beings may be more of a delicate balancing act than previously thought, with a good electrical balance just as important as a good chemical one.

The recent craze of "getting in touch with our bodies/ourselves" shows how far we've come from the belief that science can render all necessary remedies to maintain health and we need only be passive non-participants in the process. "Take a pill" is being replaced with "eat a healthier diet and get some exercise." There is a general feeling of wanting to take back control of our lives even if we don't know how or why we lost it.

Taking responsibility for our own health is essential. Even though we must rely on the wonders of modern medicine to bail us out when we suffer major trauma, proper "self-help" may eliminate the need in the first place. When it's time for a coronary by-pass, you need the surgeon, but it's better yet not to need the by-pass.

Proper exercise and diet play vital roles in maintaining proper health, but what about proper attitude? Even if we're following an exercise/diet regimen to the letter, and taking all the proper vitamins, stress could still properly kill us. Once again, the mind and the body are a team, totally interactive and cohesive in nature, not some amalgamation of individual systems which operate independently. How we "feel" is frequently more influenced by our attitude about ourselves, positively or negatively, than by any strictly physical condition.

What if we were able to gauge our health on a day-to-day basis by what we "see" as well as what we "feel"? Not just how we looked physically in the mirror, but how we saw ourselves, how we felt about ourselves. What if you used your new found auric ability to see how you felt in a whole new way? You might, for example, be a "winter" person because of the physical coloration of hair, skin and eyes, but you're really a "summer" being with fire and radiance in your aura. No wonder "winter" clothes don't look good on you! You've been ignoring the most powerful aspect of your physical presentation - the color and radiance of your own aura.

You can see what other people feel about you when you look at your aura in the mirror. They may not be consciously aware that they're sensing it, but that's what so called good or bad "vibes" are really all about. And since you now know this little secret, you've got the power to change your own auric presentation through good thoughts, emotions, meditation or prayer and consciously qualify what you see and feel about other people by viewing their aura.

It will take many years, but a time might come when seeing auras will be as commonly practiced and accepted as it seems to have been in antiquity. Wouldn't it be wonderful if we as humans re-develop these skills to the point that we can "see" when someone tells a lie because they turn suddenly a dark shade of green? Or, know when someone we love is about to be ill as their aura becomes gray?

Perhaps illness itself will be less prevalent once we become attuned to seeing these subtle electrical changes before the illness has a chance to manifest in the body. With love as the prevailing positive energizer, healing of self and others will become the norm not the rare exception through the use of Bio-Energy transfer.

# VIII

## Professional Auras

Even though everyone's aura is unique, with practice you will begin to see patterns emerge in the colors of similar types of individuals. Teaching in a large classroom environment, and later out in the world, certain students were excellent "teachers" in that they exhibited particular qualities that with experience soon became easily assigned to a profession or lifestyle. Engineers or nurses, secretaries or artists, doctors, lawyers, farmers and musicians all have different types of auras, showing colors and shapes that can sometimes be recognizable as belonging to those professions.

A little game we'd play in class was "pin the profession on the aura." After a brief description of what color was, and what part of the body each color affected, I'd attempt to guess each person's job based on the colors and intensities exhibited.

Some are easy to guess.

Although they never showed up in their "scrubs," nurses are almost invariably that very same color, aqua green, and this is due to their role as "care - givers." One nurse was so "green" that many people in the audience saw her color immediately and remarked about how uniform and bright the shape and intensity of this color was. She possessed a luminous pastel green aura, but was wearing a brown jacket over a tan sweater. I asked her to remove the jacket to see if that would make any difference, and in fact this did increase, but not change, the color.

Knowing that green is the color of balance and healing, centered as it is on the thyroid area in the upper thoracic region and neck, it was no surprise to me when she admitted that she had been a nurse for 18 years, with the last 6 being in private duty at the homes of invalids. Green, in the lighter shades, is always a sign of a harmonious and healing nature and is very commonly found in the nursing profession. This is also considered a neutral color in the spectrum as it appears between the "hot" colors of red, orange and yellow, and the "cool" colors of blue, violet and purple.

A correlation can also be drawn between green and the musical key of "F" major. Many composers used certain keys to paint a particular musical "color" and thought that sound had an effect on the soul. For example, Beethoven's "Pastoral" Symphony #6 is in the key of "F". Color is vibration on the visual level, just as musical tones are vibrations registered by the ear. It is certainly conceivable that these various vibrations do have resonant, or sympathetic, vibrations in different parts of body and soul.

Surprising then, is the fact that most doctors are dark blue or violet. At first glance you'd think that doctors would be even more green than nurses, but if you think about their differing roles in health care, it actually makes sense. Doctors utilize more brain power in their line of endeavor, outsmart the illness, or applying some chemical or mechanical fix to the problem. Their method is rigorously taught and tested in a cerebral environment, and dispassionately dispensed in hospital operating rooms where emotions would inhibit their effectiveness. Blue, being the cooler color of the mind and intellect makes perfect sense for doctors since so much of their energy is expended in thought. The serious nature of their work can cause an abundance of dark blue or indigo to manifest in their inner aura - colors which are located in the region of the head.

A friend of mine who lived across the street from my little apartment in Georgetown was a young resident surgeon who frequently enthused about the joys of cutting into people.

"Any good surgeon loves to cut. You have to really want to do it to be any good at it". He would regale me with various cases and seemed to enjoy watching me squirm as he described in graphic detail some of his operating room exploits. His aura would appear bright yellow and glow as he got more and more worked up about how he loved to "slash for cash". I could readily see in his aura how much he enjoyed his work - yellow being the color of joy and vibrancy affecting the heart/solar plexus region in the body.

Then one day I saw him, and he was uncharacteristically subdued - his aura a heavy grey - and his mood pensive. He had been present and assisted in the operation of William Casey, the Director of the CIA. The operation had not gone as expected and instead of removing a simple tumor, the team of surgeons had discovered a spreading lymphoma, the bulk of which was located in the brain's speech center "... which we totally removed."

When I remarked that the Washington Post had printed the same day on the front page that the operation was a success and Casey (involved in the Iran-Contra affair) would return to work in two to four weeks, he quietly countered, "He'll never get to testify, in fact, he'll never say another word . . . we took all that part out . . . he'll be dead within 6 months."

His assessment turned out to be accurate, and I never saw that same joyful yellow aura again. He'd become mostly grayish blue, showing lighter colors only when playing Gershwin on the piano. It's as if the seriousness of his profession had begun to wear him down, his supreme self confidence tempered by the rude intrusion of mortality. Rather than go on to specialize in neurosurgery which had always been his plan, he remains in general practice today.

Another natural profession for "blue" individuals is engineering and science. Having worked as a technical recruiter for several years in the Defense and Aerospace industry, I've been in a wonderful position to view these kinds of people. I make it a point to have a white board on the wall behind the interview chair, and have seen literally thousands of applicants in this environment. Of course there are exceptions, but in the vast majority the color that is most prevalent is some shade of blue.

Engineers tend to have a light almost sky blue and this can be very close to the head. Fuzzy or milky in nature, this shows the mind in the process of problem solving. When colors are opaque, it denotes unresolved situations, or struggle. As the color becomes clearer, a more complete or settled nature is evident. Transparency is a sure sign of attainment of goals, or closure in some endeavor. For some reason, this clarity is rare, particularly in young scientists and engineers.

Not only is the color indicative, but the shape of the aura is related to certain professions as well. Unusual, for all but engineers, is the square or box halo.

One of the most dramatic examples of this was witnessed by an entire class, as I had them write down what they saw without any prior commentary on my part. This person had a perfectly square aura which extended laterally out the left side of the head, and was dark blue in color. As the class began to see it, murmurs and exclamations could be heard throughout the room. I "shushed" them and told them to draw or write about what they saw.

Fully three quarters of the nearly 60 people in the room had drawn the box out the left side of the head and written the color as blue or violet. Again there was no surprise when he said he was the head of an architectural firm in Washington. He certainly had geometric shapes firmly in mind that night!

The only other box shape I've seen that was so perfectly angular was that belonging to my teacher, Mietek Wirkus. Actually two boxes, a small one close to the left side of his head and extending 3 or 4 inches above the center and proceeding across the top of his head in a straight line out about one foot on the side. A much bigger box was seen rising in a straight line, perhaps 2 feet above the center line of his head and extending out the right side, filling up that side of the room.

I have never seen an aura like this, before or since, and is very unusual because most auras are rounded and conform more or less to the outline of the body. The color was what you'd expect for a healer though: golden green or chartreuse and very solidly vibrant.

I don't know what these shapes mean. Perhaps it has to do with special gifts or unique brain wave activity. Maybe caused by some injury or physical quirk, they are notable in their extreme rareness, however the individuals superficially show no outward signs of abnormality. Also peculiar is the fact that I've only seen them on people involved in the engineering profession, with the sole exception of my teacher. The triangle, or "dunce cap," is much less rare, but also somewhat unusual. This has been seen numerous times in class, and usually seems to be either golden, or violet/purple in color. No pattern of lifestyle or professional association is apparent, however some subjects report higher than normal awareness of spiritual matters or psychic phenomenon. I myself have been told by some of my students that I appear on occasion to have a triangular light above my head, or sometimes rays of light pointing up in a wedge shape, or inverted triangle.

This triangle shape is most often noted in my auric field when I'm rested and non-stressed, frequently right after an extended prayer or meditation period. Colors seem more vibrant at that time as well, tending toward bright yellow or gold in the etheric (inner) aura and purple in the astral (secondary) field.

Standing in front of the class, breathing deeply and thinking loving thoughts, I can feel the warmth spreading throughout my body, with a tingling sensation shooting up my spine, energizing my hands and head. As this rush of energy develops, some members of the class will start to remark about shapes or rays of golden or silver light seen extending far above and around my body. When the feelings start to subside, often someone will remark at that moment how the "light has been turned off" and the aura changes shape or color and reverts "back to normal."

Whatever that is.

# IX

## Spiritual Auras

One truly gifted woman who has been aware of auras for over 30 years started by studying plants. She developed a keen sense of awareness by using small dense plants and shrubs as her subjects. The field is very stationary and uniform, and although more subtle than human's auras, easy to see.

Try it.

Place a healthy small plant on a table near a light. Once again you must focus past the plant either on another part of the table or a wall behind it. You should notice a fuzzy light green envelope around the outline where leaves and air meet. The more dense and healthy the plant, the brighter the aura, and therefore easier to see.

It's also fun to see the effect of various substances placed in the plant's proximity. Once you've established a base line aura, try placing a (thin) glass of red wine very near but not in the plant's field. Within a minute or two you should notice more vibrancy and some growth in the auric field of the plant. It might actually appear to "reach out and touch" the glass, as if the plant wanted to drink! Unless the plant is very dry, this won't happen if the glass is filled just with water. Try placing anything magnetic near the plant, and you'll see an opposite effect. Most metal substances will cause a similar but lessened "turning away" by the plant. This is the same reaction we see in humans when confronted with these objects. If the magnetic force is strong enough, the aura will be completely "devoured" and totally disappear!

Plants can also be useful as practice objects for viewing when people aren't around. My friend who learned how to see auras by viewing plants swears that this is the easiest and best way to learn. She has one of the most developed abilities in aura reading that I've ever encountered so who am I to argue with success? Perhaps having actively used this talent for more than 30 years also plays a part in enhancing her remarkable ability, but she still spends some time viewing various plants as well as people.

On one occasion when she was viewing my aura, she remarked about "balls of light - golden light - hovering above" my head and over my shoulders. On another occasion she says she saw "luminous figures - spirit guides I think - but definitely three beings on either side and behind" me. During yet another viewing some months later she was sure she saw "the outline of a figure - very large - directly in back of and surrounding" my image.

I finally asked her what these figures meant, and was this not unusual since she often said she saw beings around me. "Not unusual for you, it seems; I see them around many people."

Her answer startled me because I had never witnessed these phenomenon in other people before.

Now she's telling me she sees them all the time.

I don't know what to make of all this. It is possible that she is clairvoyant and that truly clairvoyant people just see these figures as a matter of course. She wasn't surprised or perturbed by their appearance, calling them "spirit guides" at one point. And since I remember seeing "guardian angels" as a child, perhaps I shouldn't be too worried. Maybe this is another natural talent we all have at birth which gets lost or forgotten as we become culturally and societally indoctrinated. Clairvoyance might be a "remembrance" of these lost natural powers which reside in some of us more readily than others.

What I do know is that the basic talent is still in all of us, one which allows us to see an aura. In fact, we're seeing auras all the time ourselves, just not consciously aware of the fact. It's only when we turn off the rational cognitive part of our brain that we can let the intuitive part "see" the human energy field. Colors (and certainly other "beings") won't be visible to everyone, but I've never met anyone who couldn't at least see the field around the head and shoulders after a minute or two of practicing the techniques while viewing one or two subjects in the proper light.

Even under less than optimum conditions (neon or fluorescent light, patterned or colored wall paper background, too close proximity to the subject), a majority of "first timers" will still see something.

Frequently, I have proven this to skeptics who, like myself many years ago, don't believe this is possible. We'll pick out a person seated some distance away at a restaurant or in a public place, and without being too obvious, "unfocus" on their aura. While not always successful, it works more often than not.

This is much easier to do in a classroom environment, where the teacher will be speaking and thus be easier to see, probably with better lighting and a more conducive viewing background.

Church is also likely to provide a peaceful viewing environment, and as the sermon is being delivered, you should have a wonderful opportunity to see "rays" or fully energized fields around the speaker, especially if the talk is devoutly delivered. People called to the priesthood should have spiritual characteristics which will be manifest in the aura. Truly religious ones, no matter what denomination or faith will show colors higher up on the frequency scale, usually indigo, violet or purple. Gold or silver will be frequently mixed in as well. Remember that depictions of holy people throughout every culture have large bright silver or gold haloes, never red, brown, green or black.

Why then do priests traditionally wear black? There are both good theological and practical reasons based on wanting to appear humble, non-worldly, and above any concern for fashion or the "glorification of the flesh." The concerns of the priest should focus on the life of the spirit, and be open to its call. Black itself is not a "color" per se but the absence of colors and absorptive in nature, reflecting or resonating back no particular hue, showing no preference. On both the metaphorical and metaphysical level, black is ideal for one who prays daily "Lord fill me with Thy blessing . . . for Thou art the Light of the World." Lux aeterna luceat eis - let perpetual light shine upon them.

What about colors in priestly vestments? At different times of the year and on certain feast days one particular color is used exclusively for that day.

Red is reserved for Martyrs' feast days and Pentecost, when Christ ascended into heaven and flames appeared over the heads of the Apostles. White is for the most important events in the liturgical calendar: Easter and Christmas. Purple is used during Advent (before Christmas), and Lent, the time of self denial before Christ's resurrection (Easter). Green is used during the "balance" of the year and is the ordinary color normally seen. These colors have been used in Christian worship for almost one thousand years and methinks this didn't happen by accident.

Historically, purple has been reserved for the robes of the higher ranks in the Catholic Church and European royalty. Being "drawn toward the purple" is a very old expression denoting aspirations of upward mobility in those two hierarchical institutions. One of my Jesuit teachers of Philosophy left the Order abruptly but remained a priest so that he might follow his "call to the purple" feeling pastoral duties, not teaching, would lead him more quickly up the ladder.

Rolls-Royce Motors, automaker of choice for the Queen of England, has an exclusive color used only for the "royal coaches" which has a complex combination of colors best described as a dark reddish purple.

England is also the place where "color baths" and color meditations were quite popular as recently as the first half of this century. Many proponents of these therapies are still around today, and claim that by "bathing" in the light projected through large jars of colored water, we derive various therapeutic effects. Thinking of colors, or imagining colorful scenes in nature is reputed to have similar effects. Drinking the color-charged water is encouraged by some as well.

I have not tried working with the water, but I do know how effective color meditation can be, especially when trying to relax, or energize the mind.

Have trouble going to sleep? Concentrate on projecting a dark clear blue on the back of your closed eyelids and if you can hold onto this visualization for 90 seconds or more you will be very near to the land of nod if not already snoring.

Got a tummy ache? Concentrate on a bright vibrant orange color and your stomach should settle down.

Want a quick blast of energy and more refreshment than an hour long nap? Visualize golden yellow entering your whole body as you breath in deeply, getting rid of dark grey waste as you exhale. Breath in to a count of four, exhale to a count of four and relax without inhaling for a count of four before starting the whole process over. Do this for 10 minutes and you'll feel wonderfully rejuvenated, and as rested as if you would have spent 10 times as long sleeping.

Colors do play a major role in our lives, and affect us in many fundamental ways we may not be aware of. Learning to use color in a whole new way could have a very positive effect on our health and everyday life.

Improvement that can be seen in your aura, and felt in your body.

# X

## Charisma

As my ability to see auras has expanded over time, so too has my portfolio of interesting subjects. Having been a performing artist for almost half of my life, I worked with many famous people and came in direct contact with those reputed to possess the rarest of gifts: charisma.

What is charisma?

How do you describe it?

Who has it and how do you get it?

Some people say it's "animal magnetism." Others might describe physical attractiveness coupled with a charged and outgoing personality. Still others might not mention physical characteristics at all, but talk about a commanding "presence" which transcends personality and pulchritude.

But everyone agrees that certain people just have it, and you'll know it when you see it.

What do the auras of such people look like? First of all, not only are all charismatic people unique and not necessarily famous, not all famous people have charisma. "Some are born great, some achieve greatness, and some have greatness thrust upon them," but Shakespeare could just as easily have described the various ways one might attain charisma. There is no set pattern or color similar to what I've noticed in other groups of people (e.g. engineers and nurses), each in some way exhibits a power or control over themselves and others. This usually goes beyond sheer ego, which should not be confused with charisma, and registers much lower in energy and color, especially when compared with true charisma.

Some families have several members, each of whom exhibit some form of this special gift. One may be "born great" due to the notoriety of the parents, one may "achieve greatness" throughout their life, and yet another may have "greatness thrust upon them."

I've had the opportunity to view such a family with all these gifts in one place and at one time, spread across three generations: Janet Auchincloss, her daughter Jackie Onassis, and her granddaughter Caroline Kennedy.

Almost by accident, I happened to be present at a family gathering to celebrate the christening of Janet Auchincloss' great grand niece at "the Yellow House" at Hammersmith Farm in Newport, Rhode Island during the America's Cup races in the late summer of 1983.

Being one of the three non-family members present in a group of about two dozen, I was the guest of Jamie Auchincloss, whom I knew through a mutual friend in Washington, D.C. This friend, myself, and the Priest who performed the Baptism were given a rare glimpse inside their world, and during the course of the day, I was able to observe the similarities and differences of these women in a variety of settings.

I was to perform at the gathering after the ceremony, but due to complications, was merely a guest all that day at the house and later that afternoon at their private beach. I was invited back to perform for a large outdoor picnic three days later, giving me another opportunity to view them and many others, royalty included.

That day of the christening however, turned out to be the perfect environment to watch three generations of "great" women. Since I didn't have to "work" the party, I was free to meet and observe them at home in a very relaxed environment. So relaxed in fact that I saw Jackie "with greatness thrust upon her" thrust a piece of christening cake into her sister Lee's face, as one was being smashed into her own, both women laughing and screaming like school girls.

As they regained their composure, the differences in aura between them was striking: Jackie by far the more radiant, Lee more reserved and darker. If anything, Lee showed more ego and Jackie more charisma. There was a shadow or darkness surrounding Lee which seemed totally absent from her sister. This was contrary to what one might assume knowing the historical facts surrounding Jackie, but she was yellow, gold, and pink alternating with purple, all of which was quite bright and clear in tone.

The kaleidoscopic nature of her aura that day was most impressive, and denotes a very complex, yet good-hearted person. There were elements of shyness (pink) coupled with strong religious reserves (purple) supported by an intrinsic sense of love and caring (yellow) and high personal attainment with control mentally, emotionally and spiritually (gold).

On the personal level, Jackie was somewhat abstract and distant, much like her daughter Caroline who was "born great." As she lay reclining on the patio chaise-lounge near the corner of the house, off by herself observing the gathering, she seemed very ethereal. I remember how translucent she looked, in a way almost ghostly, with pastel colors surrounding her head and shoulders in a tight chartreuse and pale blue band. Whereas her mother's eyes were constantly changing, never fixing her gaze too long on one spot, Caroline had a steady penetrating look of intelligence and total composure. But she too seemed remote.

For at least half an hour she remained undisturbed and I couldn't help but glance over frequently fighting the urge to walk over and talk to her. She had charisma all right, but it almost seemed to trap her in a crystalline shell, isolating her and discouraging any approachment.

My friend who for many years had openly talked of meeting her and fantasized about marrying her in order that together they might rekindle Camelot, was frozen in his tracks unable to approach the object of so many of his desires. He is not normally the retiring type, having been a Green Beret A-Team Commander in Vietnam and a survivor of polio. Such was her power of presence however, that he and I and everyone else there kept a respectful distance even after she arose and went into the house. I only ever saw her talk to her aunt and grandmother, for whom she seemed to have a great love.

But who couldn't love Janet? So accessible, warm and gracious, she made me feel I was truly welcome, and seemed genuinely interested in me and my musical career. Achieving greatness through a series of marriages to famous and powerful men, and giving birth to arguably the most admired woman on the planet, Janet Auchincloss was the matriarch of all she surveyed that day and was herself a fascinating study.

She possessed an amber and orangish aura which shows vitality and physical energy coupled with a warm personality. There was also a golden glow which seemed to spread around her and extended quite far into the room.

To a greater degree than anyone else there, she drew people toward her with this soft and comforting radiance.

Surrounded by family, standing near the back door leading to the patio, with the soft afternoon light illuminating her, Janet seemed almost regal in composure and I was struck with the feeling that she came from a different age and belonged to a different time. Perhaps in later years her progeny will take on this same aura of supreme generosity and placid majesty, but on this day, at least, her aura was unsurpassed in grace and true charisma.

Comparing their auric personalities shows Jackie to be the most complex, exhibiting fire and brilliance, with many colorful facets, much like a diamond. She was also the most mercurial, but in a totally controlled way. Caroline was intelligent and reserved, placid and composed, with lots of higher level energy held in check. She exuded a quiet and cool demeanor that was in no way snooty, but somehow failed to ignite any desire for closeness, and was the least approachable person in that group. Janet was just the opposite, perhaps because this was her house and she was most in her element, surrounded by her brood on a beautiful day celebrating a joyous occasion.

All three were quite different but each one in her own way practically defined the term charisma.

There are also famous people who come to mind who are not particularly charismatic. Some European royalty I met at parties the following week fit that description. Prince Michael of Kent was a very down-to-earth sort of fellow, that is after he got out of his hot air balloon. He seemed quite normal and approachable, with a ruddy brown and orange aura. I saw him only briefly and was introduced to him just before I began to perform but didn't note any special magnetism at that time.

Prince Johannes Thurn-und-Taxis of Bavaria was also less than electric when we met at the picnic on the hill of Hammersmith Farm overlooking the sailing ships. I saw him on three occasions that week at America's Cup parties in Newport and was invited to play aboard his ocean-going yacht for one of them. At no time did he display anything remotely resembling charisma, but rather seemed decadent and egotistical. It was very hard to see any aura at all on him, but what was there was very dark and broken, close to the body and dull. This is the same type of aura one can see on a depressed or chemically dependent person, someone with the weight of the world on their shoulders. I'm not suggesting he was any of these things, after all, who could be depressed with a net worth in the billions. Perhaps he was physically ill and taking some form of medication which will greatly affect the aura in a negative way.

Certainly the mood was festive on board the yacht that night of his party, with many glittery people in tuxedos and fancy ball gowns running around in their stocking feet so as not to mar the bleached teak deck. People seemed to be having the time of their lives as I walked around strumming my guitar and taking requests in my stocking feet.

Stopping at one table to play a request from a beautiful young woman, I was quite intrigued by her fiery aura. The lights were soft candles and the background was a freshly painted white bulkhead, so the aura was easily seen.

I found out later as I moved off to another table that the woman was Princess Gloria, Thurn-und-Taxis' wife. She was reputed to have as much royal lineage as Prince Johannes, and was quite young and beautiful. Later we talked briefly and she was surprisingly up-to-date on the American music scene, requesting several songs which I was happy to play for her.

Her aura, which I vividly remember, was like a candy cane with each of the different colors banded together. This type of aura is also rarely seen, usually appearing in children or teenagers of European ancestry, sometimes in adults of pure African or Indian stock. I've seen it in white adult males only three times, but never before this night in a white adult female.

That she was female was never in question, being the belle of the ball well into the early hours when I was finally dismissed and taken back to Hammersmith Farm where I was staying. I saw her again later that week at a dinner party hosted by "Foxy" Carter, then CIA Director of Operations in South East Asia, at their home in Newport. She was only slightly less vibrant than she had been the night on the yacht, but as I was busy entertaining in a more formal dining environment, there was a lot less opportunity to study her in depth.

Princess Gloria, perhaps due to her youthfulness and sizeable age difference with Prince Johannes, seemed to possess quite a vibrant and unique aura, very different from his. She was the only person of royal lineage I have seen who displayed characteristics which could be called charismatic.

It is important to reiterate that fame and charisma don't always mix. There must have been at least one person in everyone's family that has that special quality, or someone known to you at some time in your life be it a teacher or schoolmate, perhaps someone you work with who displays this quality. In almost every case this person will not have had an instantly recognizable public profile, but this in no way diminishes the gift they so readily display.

Some entertainers that I've worked with are all but unrecognizable off stage. But put them in lights with thousands of adoring fans, and a stunning transformation occurs.

# XI

## Aura In Performance

In the parking lot backstage standing between two semi-tractor trailer rigs wearing cut-offs and a white tee shirt, some tall gangly man was blocking my way. His long arms were spread straight out, palms flat against the aluminum sides in what could have been thought of as a menacing pose were it not for his goofy grin and flamingo like stance.

"What's in the case?" he said with apparent interest.

"Damn," I thought, "another nosey roadie" and all I want to do is get backstage and set up. I was late for sound check and didn't have time to show off my custom built guitar to another grungy stage hand.

But he wasn't moving to let me pass, and now more than half way down the tunnel formed by the proximity of two long trailers, I had no choice. Putting the case down and opening the lid we both dropped down to one knee as I carefully withdrew the instrument and handed it to him.

"Oh my God! I've never seen anything like this before. What the hell is it? Did you make this?" It was the typical reaction whenever anyone at all interested in musical instruments first sees an A.B. Adams acoustic guitar, and frankly I got tired of repeating the litany of all the wonderful details concerning its construction.

But he persisted. "What kind of neck is this? How did he cut it so thin? Look at that inlay. Wow! What are those diagonal braces inside the sound hole for? Does it have a pickup?"

I was really getting impatient and was about to take the guitar out of his hands when he finally coaxed the first chords out of it. We had been no further than three feet apart for perhaps two minutes and it was not until this moment of musical epiphany that it slowly dawned on me that this was none other than the man who had been on the cover of Time magazine. He was the maker of some of my favorite music. In fact, I knew how to play almost all of his songs by heart and owned every one of his records. I'd looked at his face on the cover of those records and magazines for years. And yet I had no idea that this unpretentious and gentle guy kneeling in front of me was James Taylor until he started to play my guitar in his signature style.

Maybe my first impression was misguided by how and where he was standing and by what he wore. It might have been due to my own focus and concentration or nervousness. The expectations of what he would be like after all those years of knowing him only through his music could have played a part also.

But the fact was, his off-stage personality and demeanor or "vibe" were more like that of a roadie or stage hand, and not at all like the internationally renowned rock star and founder of the singer/songwriter movement which in fact, he was. Rather than projecting energy, he seemed to be internalizing his forces and was on the shy side. This held true each of the several times that I saw him, and although his mood was changeable, occasionally edging toward somewhat somber, he was unfailingly gracious.

On this first meeting however, he was incredibly open and enthusiastic, telling me many personal intimacies and asking me for advice on topics such as marriage and children. He alluded to an impending divorce which shocked me since the whole world at that time believed his union with Carly Simon to be firmly entrenched. Even Parade magazine proclaimed on the cover some months after that time that his "dark night of the soul" was ended, James being saved from his destructive tendencies mostly because of his wife with whom he was totally in love and the responsibilities of raising a family together.

Here I was feeling like I was on assignment for Rolling Stone magazine, except I wasn't asking any questions, he was voluntarily opening his heart and mind to me, a total stranger. That he was entrusting me with his knowledge was more than a little overwhelming, and I'm sorry to say I never got to really focus on his aura during that time backstage right before the concert.

Quite a different personality emerged once he entered the spotlight, and I was able to study him in detail from that point forward. Much more physically active on stage than I would have guessed, he seemed to draw energy from the members of his band at first and the music just flowed out of him. As the concert progressed he became more engaged with the audience, talking more between each song. Calls from the audience of "Where's Carly?" were finally answered, almost painfully, with "ah, . . she's not . . . ah . . . here". Then he launched into the next song full force, continuing to raise the tempo through three encores.

To say he was wired after the show would be an understatement, but this wasn't due to any artificial stimulants (certainly I saw none used), rather a natural euphoria that carried on well into the next morning in the hotel lounge where he played piano and jammed with the other musicians present. This was also my first real opportunity to see his aura and it proved to be a baseline for comparison in future encounters.

I could now compare his aura as well with that of his brother Livingston, whom I had known for five years previous to this first meeting with James. Both brothers were close in age, both played and sang their own songs, but at that time they were not all that close personally, Livingston perhaps feeling the burden of constantly being compared with his more famous older brother. A fine songwriter in his own right, it must have been difficult for Liv to hear audiences requesting that he play songs written by James, as they too often did back in the early days of the 1970's.

Although they shared some familiar traits physically, here was an example of two musical brothers with similar styles but very different presentations. Their differences were readily seen in the aura, and expressed in their personalities both on and off stage. Perhaps this could help explain my lack of immediate recognition when I first met James since my long relationship with Livingston might have preconditioned my expectations that their "vibes" would be more akin to each other than they turned out to be.

Whereas Livingston was gentle off stage with a light blue evenly balanced aura, he assumed a silver sparkle when he played and sang. This was changeable depending on the instrument he was playing or the song he was singing. On piano, blue became more predominant and the silver became less bright, perhaps because he was less comfortable on that instrument and had to think more about technique than when he played guitar. Remembering that blue is the color of mental energy, this reaction to increased mental activity or stress is normal and easily explained.

You might want to try this little test on yourself. Once you become comfortable with seeing your own auric colors in the mirror by focusing past the outline of your head on the background seen in the mirror, think of the multiplication tables starting with the number 6 proceeding up to the number 12. As you work harder to remember (or figure out) the answers, notice the difference in color, size and intensity of your energy field. Unless you happen to be an arithmetic wiz, this should darken, shrink and lessen the intensity of your visible auric field.

Try it with someone for whom you have already established an auric baseline, and the same results should occur. You might even see the color change to blue if the normal baseline color is relative to it on the frequency scale (green or violet). If there is blue already in the aura, an effect similar to the one seen in Livingston Taylor's performance aura should be visible.

James Taylor's aura was very dark blue to begin with and proceeded to deepen to violet whenever he became quiet or pensive. Close to the body and quite difficult to see during these times, the energy was all drawn in. Quite thoughtful and shy, he nonetheless exhibited flashes of yellow and purple as he spoke and became animated when something caught his interest.

It was the color green however he most often exemplified both on and off stage after a performance. His clear medium green color was augmented by a golden band when he was comfortably in the midst of singing his songs - whether in front of thousands of people or just a few in a private setting. Green is the color of healing and balance and perhaps this shows the therapeutic nature of his music on his own psyche.

He exhibits multiple colors in the spectrum at other times and has a complex auric field. Therefore, it could be surmised that he is most happy and balanced when he's in a musical mode. Words like "warm", "smoothing", and "mellow" come to mind when one thinks of his music, far different from the well documented lifestyle of drugs and depressions that were central elements early in his life. Music undoubtedly played a role in overcoming these handicaps, and in the last several years he appears to be healthy.

Another survivor in the rock-and-roller coaster is Jerry Garcia of the Grateful Dead. Despite several near misses over the years, he manages to avoid incorporating himself too literally with the name of his band and seems to be flourishing on several levels. Making a name for himself in the art world, along with marketing a line of designer apparel items, he shows himself to be a man of colors as well as sounds. Certainly he has led a very colorful life and has the aura to prove it.

Gregarious and self effacing with a strong sense of humor that creates an underlying mirthful ambience whenever I've seen him, Jerry also possesses surprising drive and intelligence. All these elements make for a complexity of aura not easy to isolate or define and I've seen such a variety of auric patterns with him it's difficult to know what is real rather than chemically induced.

When I first met him in New Haven, Connecticut in 1978, backstage before a Grateful Dead concert, he seemed almost contemplative and subdued. There were sparks of random energy coming off his head and shoulders as he stood in a corner of the large dressing room warming up, waiting to go on. But the grey paint on the cinderblock walls of the coliseum and overhead fluorescent lighting weren't ideal conditions for color determinations, and there were other members of the band I was being introduced to including Bob Weir, the other guitarist in the band, that prevented me from fully focusing on him.

Later that night after the concert back in the hotel room, I got a much better look at both Garcia, Weir, and other members of the band and retinue. Here again was perhaps a distorted picture due to the unknown influences of various substances, but both Garcia and Weir showed very strongly different vibes which were seen in their auras.

Quite complimentary in their divergence, Jerry Garcia possessed the more wide open and colorful field, with Bob Weir the more controlled and angular aura. Whereas Garcia filled a larger space with a brighter more electric and eclectic series of colors, Weir was more mono - chromatic and diffuse.

A quieter, softer radiance was Weir's, showing a steely blue gray color and a close projection off the body. Fuzzy in nature with clearly defined boundaries, his aura brought to mind words like "cautious", "controlled" and "analytical". He seemed to be quite thoughtful and he expressed himself in hesitant yet concise and logical fashion, very similar indeed to his auric presentation which mirrored the man precisely.

There were other times when I've seen him physically quite active, and almost out of control, taken to sudden bursts of energy, as if he were breaking out of some form of confinement. I haven't been able to get a steady read on his aura at these times due to such active movement, so I can't tell what color, if any, he changes into, but following such activity his aura becomes more open and vibrant, with lots of yellow (high emotions) in place of the blue.

Certainly Bobby exhibits more energy on stage than Garcia, moving around quite freely while Jerry seems rooted in one spot, content to let the music do all the movement. It's as if Weir is consciously working to physically overcome his basic auric nature, which is conservative and tightly held, and Garcia is concentrating on marshalling his more free form and expansive energies into a clearly defined focus; both fight their own natural tendencies when they play.

This holds true when both men are fronting their own personal groups as well, but to a lesser extent. Having performed as the solo opening act for Weir's band "Bobby and the Midnights" and Jerry Garcia's band "Reconstruction", I've been with each of them in several different venues where they've performed as individuals without the frenzy of a complete Grateful Dead experience, although some aspects of it are present whenever they play.

Because I've never been a "Dead Head", as their followers call themselves, I've gotten an objective look into this colorful and unique lifestyle. A direct carryover of the late 1960's, complete with tie dyed clothes and psychedelic behavior, this time-warped world is still populated by 18 year olds (. . . some as old as 60) for whom Peace and Love are still paramount.

A new generation has taken up these precepts, and recreates the hippie scene nightly with this band of originals forming the central totem. Garcia and Weir play off this energy (and each other) in a way that creates a sum much greater than their individual parts, driving and being carried along with their faithful as they play.

This synergy is totally absent when each man performs separately and lacking this friendly friction, I always felt a hollowness in their individual efforts, masked somewhat by the ever present adoring fans, but never able to take the energy into that magical realm reserved, it seems, for full communion with the Dead.

What is the magic of performance? Why do we want to be near it, to watch it and therefore take part in it? What makes one performance great and another only average? Could it be some subtle exchange of energy present in one, missing in another? Does the aura of the performer actually touch the audience?

Janis Joplin compared performing to sex - only she thought performing on stage was better! I can tell you from a performer's viewpoint, there are times when I am so in touch with an audience that feelings very similar to post coital euphoria engulf me as the waves of applause build and crest, crashing down around me. "I had that audience in the palm of my hand" must have been said by every person who ever stood in front of an audience more than once and liked it. Being on stage is either a terrifying experience you never want to repeat, or a tremendous excitement you can never forget. It all depends on forging a loving link with the audience.

A good entertainer lifts our spirits and makes us forget about our personal problems for awhile. Whether the medium is music, drama, dance, or even story telling around a campfire, the audience is drawn into the artist's world. Magic happens when the spell is cast and the artist and audience create a world together. In transcending the ordinary every day reality, artist and audience create a group aura that might be seen, (if you could get far enough away to view the group as a whole) but is definitely felt by all present.

One type of performing artist who relies totally on making and holding an immediate personal link with the audience is the comedian.

When the "vibes" don't click, it's a very painful experience for artist and audience. Usually the comedian has no place to hide, no instrument to stand behind, no song to sing, just jokes to tell that aren't very funny. Those same jokes told by another person might well be hysterically funny but only if the auric link is established with the audience first.

Even when he was just staring out as a stand-up comedian, Yakov Smirnoff had already learned this lesson naturally. A recent immigrant from what was then Soviet Russia, he learned the English language as a dishwasher at clubs in the Catskills by listening to the comedians' routines. His accent and timing were terrible, but I immediately liked something about him--his stage presence and willingness to try.

During a weekend spent together sharing the stage at a comedy club in Washington, D.C., I got to watch him hone his craft long before he was the star of his own TV show. With childlike wonder and honesty, he was still in a fresh state of cultural shock about everything American. His humor is derived from his own actual experiences both here and in Russia, so audiences are generally tolerant because of his honestly charming excitement which carries them along into his world. By humorously casting his life's tribulations, he holds up a mirror in which we view both his and our own experiences, but he makes us see our world with his Russian eyes. Yakov's real talent is the ability to create that empathy with an audience which transcends culture, language and national barrier, and he turns those tremendous potential handicaps into valuable opportunities for unity with his audience.

Every great artist presents a truth. The truth might not always be beautiful, nor will it always be immediately recognized, but when truth and beauty do come together, an ecstatic moment occurs. Ecstasy's Greek root (ek histemi) means literally "knocked out of one's stance" or roughly in today's vernacular, "blown away". Perhaps the truth can set you free in more ways than one.

Almost always, the best art has some elements of the body, mind, heart and soul present in it, no matter what the format. It draws us out of ourselves and pushes us toward a higher state of awareness and understanding by resonating with some (or all) of these aspects of our true nature. Affirmation of this nature, especially when it touches the heart and soul, is the great attraction to all manner of performing arts. Confirmation of these "ecstatic" moments is what brings us back time after time to relive the magic of this transcendent experience. Both artist and audience are fed and nurtured by this symbiotic relationship.

These empowering experiences certainly are what keeps the entertainer and audience coming back for more, and may account for some artists' incredible longevity. Comedians like George Burns, Bob Hope and Henny Youngman are all in their upper 80's and 90's--living proof that laughter can keep you young. Famous Symphonic Conductors as a group are notorious for their long lives, frequently directing orchestras well into their 80's. Only when a performer smokes themself to death (Leonard Bernstein, John Wayne) or drugs themself into oblivion (too numerous to mention) do we see less than average life spans in public performers.

So what is this energy transfer that happens on stage? We can see and feel the effects no matter what side of the stage lights we're on. Is the lack of this energy what causes so many performers to indulge in artificial stimulants?

Some lucky stars, like James Taylor and Jerry Garcia, live through their indulgences and perform at or above the level they displayed when first becoming famous, attaining a peace and tranquility along the way surprising even to themselves. Could the love and adulation they received from so many souls over such a long time have been their real saving grace?

Judy Collins, a 60's era survivor herself best known for singing "Amazing Grace" at President Clinton's inauguration, might tell you that it is. She will tell you that this is her favorite and most requested song. It has special meaning, not only for civil rights activists who used it as an anthem, but for all the survivors of that socially and politically charged time.

When I first met her as she was about to play at my college in the Fall of 1972, she was radiant, laughing, friendly and open. We played guitar together backstage before the concert and she seemed not to have a care in the world. Full of energy, she epitomized the hopes and aspirations of the "New Generation."

How different Judy looked as she walked in the stage door and trudged down the hallway to her dressing room in late January 1993. Tiny, withdrawn, and quiet, eyes darting then averting, she looked like a trapped elf. Once again, I didn't recognize someone I thought I knew.

But what a transformation when Judy "Amazing Grace" Collins hit the lights! She went from negative aura to full ecstasy faster than anyone I've ever seen. Could this really be the same person? Clearly the audience had a profound impact on her, and after the concert she radiated a silver sparkle with intermittent rays projecting almost a foot around her head and shoulders.

She talked about being "on a pink cloud" at the Inauguration, surrounded as she was by her musical contemporaries and at the head of that class. Different from a quarter century before, ("If you remember the 60's...you weren't there") this was a drug-free defining moment for her entire generation and one never to be forgotten.

Judging by her radiant aura, she had come full circle with youthful idealism and for at least that instant, Judy Collins was in the midst of an historic lovefest once again, not at Woodstock this time, but at the White House in Washington for a command performance by her biggest fan, the newly elected President of the United States, Bill Clinton.

It's hard to imagine a more wonderful feeling.

# XII

## Politically Correct Aura

Imagine then what Virginia Kelly, the mother of Bill Clinton must have felt at that moment! Having just seen her son sworn in as the 42nd President of the United States, I saw her as she was flying home to Arkansas early Sunday morning after a week of inaugural festivities that left her on "cloud 9." In fact, from what I could see, she might not have needed the airplane.

Sitting across the isle from me on flight 1661 to Nashville, I had no idea who this woman in black was. She certainly seemed well known to everyone else, shaking hands and signing autographs as she walked up and down the aisle right after takeoff. Maybe she was some old country and western singer I didn't recognize. The man next to me took a large ceramic tile button with Clinton's picture on it out of his pocket and handed it to me.

"Give this to Virginia when she comes back to sit down, I don't think she's got one of these."

Obviously I was still oblivious, so he said, trying to be helpful, "She's the President's mother you know."

Because this was a regular commercial flight and I assumed it would be unthinkable for THE President's mother not to be on AirForce One or some private jet, I honestly wondered, "why was everyone making such a fuss over the mother of the president - of what - American Airlines?"

Not until the Captain came over the loudspeaker and said "We'd like to thank the Little Rock Mafia for flying home with us today," as applause and cheers rang throughout the cabin, that reality finally dawned on me. "We're going to have to ask you to take your seats as we are about to encounter some bumpy weather which shouldn't last too long. Then you can move around the cabin again." Seems I got myself booked on the homebound Arkansas inaugural party junket by accident, and as Virginia came back to her seat, I dutifully handed her the trinket with her son's photograph emblazoned on it.

"That's my boy! That's my boy!" she squealed. "Where did you get this?" I pointed to the man on my left who gave it to me to give to her. "Say, I know you, you're Jane's husband!" At that moment she put her left hand on my shoulder and bracing herself with her other hand on the top of the seat in front of me, leaned over six inches in front of my face to commence an animated conversation with this man until the flight attendant gently insisted that she take her seat.

"Can you believe they're gonna make me sit down?" She was back up in my face leaning on my shoulder as soon as the "fasten seatbelt" sign went off. Offering to let her sit in my seat when I could get a word in edgewise, she responded with "Don't be silly, I'm perfectly comfortable!" The fact that I was not was of no consequence and after several more minutes I had wondered if the slope of my shoulder would be permanently altered.

Finally she turned and looked right at me.

"So what do you do?"

There were so many thoughts racing through my head that time slowed down to micro-second intervals. I was flabbergasted first and foremost to be face-to-face with what was a very close likeness of her son, Bill, and she possessed the most intense violet colored eyes I'd ever seen. Adding to this was the realization that I was up way too close and personal with the mother of the President and there were a lot of questions I wanted to ask her.

In response I mumbled something about performing for the Gore family the night before the Vice Presidential debates and added that "my brother Michael went to school with your son Bill at Georgetown."

"Well, I just knew you were somebody!" she said as she squeezed my shoulder a little harder.

Stifling the urge to point out that my brother had been in the Army R.O.T.C (and her son was . . .not), I did finally ask my most pressing question, "What does all this really feel like for you?"

Virginia rolled her eyes, tilted her head back and let out a yelp. Then she looked down right at me and with a beatific smile that permeated her whole being, said slowly with an almost mystical passion, "ohhhh honey . . .", words could not describe it, none in fact were necessary. Her look said it all--this was a truly transcendent moment.

How odd than that I sensed all was not well with her physically. You might think with all the peak life experiences happening for her, and all the obvious external joy and excitement that Virginia Kelly's aura would be astounding. This unfortunately was not the case.

Staying close to her body with very fuzzy and vague pastel color, her aura showed low vibrancy but a fair degree of luminosity. The color alternated from a dull burnt orange to a very light frosty blue. Sometimes the aura seemed to vanish entirely, as if the plug had been pulled out of the electrical wall socket suddenly. Then just as suddenly, it would return, glow strongly, flicker and subside, never extending more than an inch or two out from the body.

At the time, my thoughts were that she must be exhausted from so much excitement, and I was concerned about the sudden loss of power. Thinking perhaps that she might be on some kind of strong chemical therapy, there seemed to be a correlation between what she exhibited and some cancer patients I'd recently seen. Fairly typical in such cases, or when some type of radiation is used on a person, the aura shows large gaps, or is very weak and depleted, in need of major replenishment.

The treatment of cancer with its debilitating side effects can be almost as devastating as the disease, and when seen in the aura, it can be impossible to distinguish between the disease and the effects of the treatment, but I believe that whatever the cause, I saw in Virginia's aura the telltale effects of that disease.

Another woman I'd worked with about that time had an inoperable tumor in her chest. She had received massive amounts of chemo and radiation therapy, and the tumor which was pressing against her bronchial tube and aorta had reduced to the size of a baseball. When I first visited with her, she looked quite healthy outwardly and told me nothing of what was wrong with her, wanting me to discover, if I could, what her problem was. As I placed my hands around her auric field, I was surprised to find a very clearly defined area in her upper torso which literally shot out random sparks that felt like the lit end of a sparkler had been placed in my palm, only more pronounced.

This was so strong a sensation that I knew at once radiation had been recently employed, but was masking any feeling of the tumor itself.

So it was with Virginia Kelly. Although I was unable to accurately feel her aura due to the circumstances, the visible effects in the aura were quite clear even though outwardly she looked to be in the peak of health, and on top of the world.

This close encounter with the mother of the President proved to be an interesting counterpoint to my experience with the parents of the Vice President, Al and Pauline Gore. Having been with them at a dinner party just a few months before my plane ride with Bill Clinton's mom, the difference in demeanor (and aura) was striking.

Al Gore Sr. had himself been a well known politician for several terms in the Senate, and in many ways gave the impression he was the one still running for office. Here, he was in an odd situation of trying to restrain his normal flamboyance so as not to upstage his more conservative son.

Mrs. Pauline Gore was the ever dutiful wife and proud mother, presenting herself with a calm reserve, leaving the limelight for her husband and son. She was frequently referred to in her husband's speech, and used as an example of common sense and practicality in an uncommon and sometimes impractical political world. The calm eye of the swirling whirlwind, she was also reputed to be quite a comedienne. All of which seemed to make Pauline wince and squirm ever so slightly, even as she sat smiling and staring up at Al Sr. on the dais as he spoke.

When they were seated together and talking quietly, their auras could be seen to be melding together and equalizing, which frequently happens with couples married for many years. (You can see this effect yourself when practic-

ing the exercises mentioned earlier with two people standing face-to-face.) Even with individuals who are total
strangers, this coalescing effect can happen fairly rapidly,
but try it with married couples and the phenomenon should
be more pronounced.

With Albert Gore Sr. what was interesting was watching the evolution from his "at rest" aura to the various
changes that transpired throughout his speech. The effect
of an audience on the performer's aura can be readily seen
in most cases, and as he spoke, all the usual traits began to
manifest themselves such as increased glow and size, with
a color change from orange to yellow happening only after
he was more than half way into the speech.

As the former Senator became more relaxed after telling some jokes about himself and the family, he started pick-
ing up steam (and auric vibrancy) as he spoke of his onetime
political differences with his son concerning Vietnam, and
as the old stump speechmaker started heading for home
with exhortations to vote for his son, a warm golden glow
enveloped and energized both he and his wife Pauline.

After dinner, they were quite gracious and animated,
never meeting a stranger, it seemed, spending several minutes with everyone who wanted to talk with them. Now
they were inhabiting the same golden yellow bubble, even
while conversing separately with different individuals. If
not starting to physically resemble each other as some married couples do, their auras at least were well in tune with
one another, exhibiting a sum greater than (and different
from) their individual parts.

"I just can't get over having Albert on what is going
to be the winning ticket in this election. We've got to get
the Democrats back in the White House and I know he'll be
a positive influence, so you've got to get out there and

support him, support the whole ticket, bring Alabama in as a State that voted Democratic . . ." Even off the podium, his blood was up and the fire was still burning. Hopes were rising and the polls looked good if only they could carry this momentum through to victory.

There was the strangely tentative sense of victory in the air, almost as if everyone was afraid to really believe it, lest defeat be snatched from the jaws of apparent victory. After all, Jimmy Carter and Walter Mondale were the last Democratic ticket voted into the White House and that was 16 long years ago...

Twelve years before, I had witnessed this scene in reverse.

Just after the Carter/Mondale defeat in 1980, I was invited to Walter and Joan Mondale's house for dinner by the girl I was dating, the daughter of a Democratic representative from Maine. Melissa and I, along with her sister and date, were at the Mondale's with Bronson Clark, the girls' father.

We talked about everything but politics before dinner, focusing on Joan's extensive collection of modern and post modern American Art. She really loved these works by Motherwell, Rothko and de Kooning, glowing with a close to the body but bright and fuzzy pink aura as she took us on a tour of the house. This was the most animated and happy she appeared to be all night, her aura increasing in size and radiance as she spoke about each piece of art.

None of us really shared her level of enthusiasm, but Joan was in her own world, and seemed liberated there in her private home, away from a public life which couldn't have been much fun for her at that time. As a patron of the arts, she could find solace in promoting something she truly loved, putting away any need to present a politically correct persona. The pink color she exhibited showed a pure heart and an air of innocence at least while she was surrounded by the art that provided a refuge from the political reality of the moment.

As dinner progressed she seemed to recede in vibrancy, and after dinner as the talk gradually began to touch on politics, Joan seemed abstract and withdrawn, adding very little if anything to the discussions. A forced air of conviviality predominated the remainder of the evening, conversations taking on a leaden inevitability with the focus subtly shifting toward finding out about who this boyfriend of Melissa's was.

Rather than ask me directly how I voted in the most recent election just past, derisive comments were made and jokes told about Nixon's failed presidency with all eyes watching my reaction. If I had shared their scathing sentiments, I presumably would have passed the test.

After baiting me repeatedly, but failing to bite, it was Joan who finally let me off the hook as she turned away suddenly and said, "So tell me Bronson, how's the fishing up in Maine?"

Thankful to have escaped further scrutiny, I was overcome by a greater sense of elation when leaving than arriving. Not that the evening hadn't been enjoyable, but the combination of election loss and the resultant underlying mood made for a challenging experience, poles apart from the feeling of impending victory I'd experienced with the soon-to-be Vice Presidential family more than a decade later.

Politics varies from entertainment in several fundamental ways (although they've been compared more directly since the election of our first actor/president).

If a performer has an off night, there's always tomorrow. When a politician loses, it can be years, if ever, before vindication occurs.

It is no wonder then, that the aura of politicians tends to be very different from that shown by entertainers. When actually giving a speech, a politician is performing, and subject to the audience/actor dynamic, but that is where the similarity ends. Politicians I've seen up close, whether winners or losers, show a darker, deeper shade of whatever color they radiate, (frequently navy blue) and seem very controlled and compact in radiance, extending no more than one or two inches.

# XIII

## Aura Near Death

One of the most talked about phenomena in the last quarter century is the near death experience (NDE), during which someone dies, or appears to be close to death, yet returns to this life with stories about a "world beyond." An estimated thirteen million people in this country alone have had this startling experience. Many books, movies, magazine articles and TV shows have examined NDE's or other "out-of-body" (OBE) experiences which don't involve actual "clinical" death but are similar in nature. The real number of experiences is likely even greater since many people are reluctant to talk about something so extraordinary and unbelievable that "normal" people might think them crazy.

Reports of these experiences tend to follow many if not all of these common threads:

1) A sense that the "person" has left his or her body and is floating directly above it.

2) An omniscient view of the area, with a detailed understanding of what is being done by others present, especially common during emergency medical procedures, or surgery.

3) Passing through a tunnel or dark space toward a bright light.

4) Finally arriving at the "loving light" which is indescribably radiant and warm, "attractive" and supremely peaceful.

5) Full knowledge and understanding of everything. You become part of the universe and know your place in it.

6) Seeing others, some whom you might recognize as deceased family members or friends.

7) Watching a vivid movie of your life "pass before your eyes" highlighting both the positive and negative aspects contained therein.

8) A realization that this is not yet your time to go, or the feeling of "coming to the end of your (cosmic) rope", at which point you suddenly

9) Return to your body.

The actual duration of the experience in temporal time might be for only a few seconds, or could last an hour or more in rare cases. But to the experiencer, there is no correlation to time as we know it. In fact, there is very little correlation to anything we think we know in our normal reality.

Words can't describe these "out-of-body" experiences any better than we can describe color to a blind person, or music to a deaf-mute. Imagine what it would be like to have lived in a cave your whole life, then suddenly find yourself outside in the warm sunlight surrounded by oceans and mountains, farmlands and forests, experiencing all of this simultaneously for the first time in a kaleidoscopic panoply. Then having to go back to your cave and explain it all to the others who know life only as it exists inside that cave.

Even this analogy does not fully describe the overwhelming sensory and emotional overload caused by these experiences.

Common initial responses given by most OBE and NDE individuals when asked to relate what happened during their "trip" are:

"Words can't describe it at all."

"Language is inadequate to convey the feelings."

"You've got to experience it, then you'll know."

"It's like nothing in this world."

"I can't put it in words, but I didn't want to leave!"

NDE and OBE often cause life altering behavioral changes in those who have the experience. Perhaps OBEs are even responsible for many mystical/religious conversions, such as St. Paul's epiphany on the road to Damascus when he encountered "the light" and became a follower of Christ instead of a persecutor of Christians. In fact, the Bible is full of mystical experiences which could be attributed to some type of OBE. Mystics of all religious faiths speak of transcending earthly bounds, glimpsing heaven briefly then returning to speak of the wonders they have seen. Universal truth, beauty, wisdom and above all, the unlimited power of love resonate through these experiencers who might use their cultural traditions or religious beliefs to describe and personify this "loving light" as a manifestation of God.

Most people who have these experiences don't set out to save the world, but they do gain a different perspective on life. Some actually withdraw from previous career paths, or change directions toward service for others rather than continue to chase financial or material accumulation of wealth.

Many NDE experiencers report profound changes in their attitude toward people in general, and family and friends in particular. Having glimpsed the "Big Picture," emotions such as fear, impatience, and hostility usually cease to be of concern for these people, and these sometimes radical changes can be mystifying for those around them.

One of the greatest benefits of the NDE/OBE experience is the elimination of fear, particularly the fear of death. Everyone whom I have spoken to, or read about or seen on TV who has had these experiences tells of this liberation from the fear of dying. We might not lose the fear of pain and suffering, or the sense of grief and loss when someone close to us dies, but the actual transition out of this life no longer causes any fear or dread. For many experiencers, the idea of death can almost be described in terms of "going home."

While there is no longer a fear of dying, there seems to be no increase in wanting to die among experiencers. Research done on the case histories of NDE among suicide attempts shows a zero incidence of repeat attempts. That is, those who had the near death experience while attempting to commit suicide have all subsequently chosen to live, while non NDE suicides continue at the normal repeated attempt rate of 80%. There are more than 100 people included in this ongoing study by Dr. Bruce Grayson at the University of Connecticut which tracked the lives of these suicide attempt NDEs over a time period of as long as 20 years. Whatever happens to people who have these experiences (which science is still at a loss to explain), the data certainly indicated profound changes in behavior and lifestyle.

Rather than choose to die, near-death and out-of-body experiencers become more attuned to life. Each day becomes more intense, relationships grow more intimate, time more precious. Many NDEs report that the love and needs of their children or some unfinished business with family members as the primary factor in their return to this existence. There is a reason why we are here, (although the specifics may still be hidden from us after a near-death experience), and it is this sense of "mission" that intensifies our lives after NDE/OBE, and prevents us from "checking out" of this life prematurely.

In my own case these experiences have had a profound impact, and perhaps due to their early and frequent occurrence, I've always felt "directed" and very blessed. Even as a small child there was an awareness and acceptance of a "world beyond." This strong link with spirituality was reinforced by a 1950's era Catholic school education. Yet I was rebellious and considered "different" by my grade school peers. My parents might say "difficult", but curiosity about almost everything I encountered led me into the trouble in which I frequently found myself. After deciding at age 11 that I had an unlimited potential (and strong attraction) to commit mischief, I also knew that I was on earth to utilize my talents for positive purposes, and pledged to do so one spring night as I lay in bed thinking and praying just before my twelfth birthday.

Each successive out-of-body experience made me more aware of my "calling" which has now led me through several changes of careers and various geographic locations. Having been fortunate enough to successfully experience life from many perspectives, I've never felt limited or lonely, just lucky and loved.

Even though I've never married or found my "soul mate," I have had some wonderfully deep and passionate relationships. Every friend or lover has taught me something, but I guess I'm still supposed to continue to learn. I do feel the need to have a child and hope one day to have this paramount life experience, but that event might not be "called" for. Perhaps the NDE/OBEs I've had are the only (re-)birth experiences I will ever know and if so, my life has been and continues to be extraordinarily full and happy.

Were the NDE/OBEs the primary cause of this happiness? I don't think so, but they did offer a particular insight which certainly helped me overcome setbacks enabling me to place failures and disappointments in a larger perspective.

Did these out-of-body experiences change my ability to see auras? Again, I don't think so, because anybody can see the aura, not just NDE/OBE experiencers.

Will the aura change after this type of experience? It probably does, but I've never done a before-and-after study. I can say that the auras of people I've met individually or at near-death and out-of-body symposiums who have had these experiences seem to be a little brighter and more radiant than the average person I might see on the street or in one of my classes, for instance. There is something about a person who has had this type of experience that might not be readily apparent at first, but as the conversation turns to subjects relating to certain topics (spirituality, life after death, philosophy, states of consciousness, etc.), an almost agitated level of enthusiasm can frequently be noticed. This excitement is what causes the higher energy display seen in the aura, and is a major factor in an NDE/OBE aura.

And yet there is an uncommon sparkle that these people show in their auric field which is in some ways similar to that previously described as belonging to charismatic people. The difference seems to be in the frequency of the vibration, with the charismatic person exhibiting a slower, lower, more physically exciting vibration, while the NDE/OBE "vibe" is faster, clearer and more ethereal.

Although there doesn't seem to be a particular color associated with either NDE/OBE or charismatic persons, the color they do possess is quite bright and radiant. The quality of the energy projected in the aura seems more focused or clear, and frequently there seems to be much more quantity as well.

Some aura "readers" and psychics don't actually see colors when they view the auric field, they base their often startling insights only on the "energy level" they see and feel.

Recently my aura was "read" by one such person who didn't know that I was writing a book on the subject. In fact, she knew nothing about me at all.

She sat me down in her naturally lit office in front of a white shower curtain. Referred to her by one of my students, I was fascinated to see just what someone else's technique for viewing auras would be like, and judging from her set up and professional environment (no incense, hanging beads or gypsy costumes) we were off to a good start.

This woman then told me that she only interpreted the energy a person projected and did not see colors in the aura at all.

Then she proceeded to tell me several details of my recent past which were too specific (and accurate) to be coincidental. "I see you've been in a dentist's chair recently but haven't been here in a long time. You're also going back again next week."

That was true. Two days prior I'd had a molar temporarily crowned on my first visit to a dentist in almost three years and was returning for the permanent crown in less than a week.

"Do you have sinus problems?"

I said no.

"I'm getting a sinus drainage and I don't have any allergies or a cold myself, so if you don't have the problems, someone close to you does." I thought a minute and remembered that my girlfriend was a chronic sinus and upper bronchial inflammation sufferer but before I could say anything she said, "You are in close personal or work related contact with two women who have this problem." Then I remembered that my secretary had left work early just the previous day with a severe case of sinusitis. She continued before I could respond, "One of the women is about to make a big change. I see her taking off a badge with her picture on it, and moving far away." She pantomimed the action of unclipping the badge and held it out as if she should give it to me.

I realized this was true as my secretary was in her last month of work, about to move to another state due to her husband's transfer and that I, as the Staff Human Resources person, would take her badge as she processed out of the company.

Clearly, something special was happening here, and she was on a roll. But how could she be "seeing" this from an aura? I certainly couldn't foretell the future or describe the recent past by looking at an aura.

Or so I thought.

After telling me I would meet my wife (how did she know I wasn't already married?) in about 18 months at a "lecture I was to give concerning a paper I had written," her husband walked into the office and handed her a message. He looked at me briefly and then left. I was struck by how white and fuzzy his aura looked and I could feel the physical and emotional pain pour radiantly off him in waves.

When my reading was over, and I told her that I too could see auras, she wanted immediately to know what I saw in her husband's aura.

"Tell me about his health . . . how long do you think he has yet to live?" Startled by her questions, I protested that I had only seen him for a few seconds, not long enough to form any in-depth opinions and certainly it wasn't a habit of mine to tell people if they were about to die. "Go on, you know very well he's ill. If you can see auras, you should be able to see his pain, its location, its intensity, and if you see that, then you'll know about the rest . . ."

As I recalled his brief entrance into the room, I saw again the white/gray aura and remembered how fuzzy he looked. Although I've never experienced it, there are various accounts of persons not boarding airplanes or elevators at the last second because they felt death was imminent, or saw in the faces of the people gathered before them something terminal. It was this same type of intuition that I must admit I felt when I thought about the man and his faint and pale aura.

Pain seemed to be radiating from him consistently and his expression could be described as a tightly controlled grimace, his posture slightly stooped, and his gait more of a shuffle than a walk. To guess his age would be difficult but it was probably lower in number than he looked. Yet this information could be readily attained by looking at the man with my regular vision. The auric characteristics were in keeping with the overall physical condition and had many of the elements present when one is about to transit from this life.

My new auric friend pressed me for more details. "When is he going to die? Weeks, months, years . . . What do you see?" Flippantly I responded, "it almost looks as if he wants to die, and very soon too, based on his white aura." White is the color of either very saintly persons, or ones about to depart this life.

"Excellent! You really do have the vision. He wanted to commit suicide last night, and I've hidden his gun again today. He's been talking about wanting to die for a while now and I'm afraid he just might do it. I've got to watch him all the time . . ."

Once again, my skepticism was confounded by the events. Trusting my instincts instead of logic allowed me to stumble into a correct assessment of a situation I would not have believed was within my power, even after I had just witnessed the same type of clairvoyant assessment done on me.

# XIV

## Reflecting On Our Aura

I've been accused of being "hard headed," but after all this time, and all these "discoveries" you'd think I'd be completely amenable to the mysteries of life, and to the possibility that we are capable of so much more than we know.

Well, I'm not totally there yet.

Unfortunately, there are many of us who are totally shut off from exploring anything new or different, especially something as different as exploring our capacity to see and feel the human aura.

That's a shame because these extraordinary capabilities, however we come by them or in whatever form they take, allow us to glimpse our transcendent spirituality, and are a foundation for our link with the Divine. Ironic then to think that the use and mastery of these talents, whether they be aura reading, energy healing, astral projection, clairvoyance, handwriting analysis, et al, are natural expressions of our human nature as well.

Most of us are searching for truth and meaning in life. As we approach the millennium some of us are becoming more concerned with deeper questions and probing past the superficial issues, interested more in root causes. The age old questions of "Who am I, and what am I doing here?" are still with us (and mostly unanswered), but are augmented by more global concerns such as "How are we going to manage to co-exist on this tiny planet without destroying ourselves and our fragile environment?" There is a growing sense that time is running out, and that we must change old habits and perceptions in order to survive.

Of course this is not true for all of us - there are the professional "naysayers."

These cynics and backward thinkers have existed in every culture, and the world today is plagued by their actions. Unfortunately some of them are in positions of power around the world. Real enlightenment rarely comes down from the top. Instead social, political, and spiritual repression are the norm rather than the exception throughout many parts of the world. Individuals progress much faster than social structures as a whole, and there must be an enormous number of frustrated individuals who are many steps ahead of their respective governments in their desire to grow and prosper. Tragically, several pockets of savagery around the world don't look like they will admit to change anytime soon.

With nationalism and even tribalism on the rise since the end of the cold war, these retro "anti-global" forces are the major stumbling block facing humanity on its inevitable path toward true global unification. China, Russia, and Japan have operated as insular societies for so long, it may be generations before nationalistic bastions such as these truly integrate with the rest of the world on all levels. Non-secular states such as Iran will take even longer.

Nevertheless, the inhabitants of these countries historically have been among the most advanced and enlightened in art, literature and philosophy. The governments of these countries, however, have been among the most repressive.

Is free thought and spiritual enlightenment an escape from social oppression? Or are repressive governments a conservative reaction to "dangerous"anarchist liberal thought? Dangerous to whom? Governments and social institutions of all types are in business to stay in business, but they might be out of business if the free thinkers of the world ever got together.

We've seen pictures taken by the astronauts that show the Great Wall of China as the only man made line of demarcation visible anywhere on the planet. Other than that, no evidence of individual countries exist on Earth when viewed from Space. Yet we have a natural inclination on Earth to think always in terms of "us" and "them."

So just imagine for a moment that UFO's really existed. I'm not saying that they do exist (remember I'm still a little skeptical), since unlike auras, I've never seen one, but suppose they landed on the White House lawn in broad daylight, and in capitals around the world.

What would be the immediate effects of such an event?

With this uncontrovertible evidence that we are not alone in the universe, do you suppose we might start to think and act more globally? When the idea sunk in that there was something DIFFERENT out there, and that the universe was comprised of more sentient species than just us, would we start to behave in a more communal fashion? Politics "as usual" would start to look awfully petty and cease to exist in short order. "Nationality" would become trivial, and would be replaced with "specialty." Concerns about Serbia vs. Croatia would be replaced by concerns about Earth vs. Alpha Centuri. Global thinking would be forced on us all. We would soon become the United States of Earth.

Maybe the citizens of planet Earth already know this intuitively. The vast majority of us believe in other life forms in the universe, even if we're skeptical of the reports of alien abductions, and flying saucers with little men in silver suits that come from a different dimension. This belief in some form of non-human life might explain our increasing cynicism about "politics as usual" and disgust at the self serving short sighted interests of many of our politicians, and world leaders.

The religions of the world as well would all loose their grip, as the various denominational differences evaporated in the face of alien epiphany. Since all religions are man made attempts to put God in a bottle, or rather, in their temple, and God has always been viewed by each religion as mankind's monogamous lover cast in their own image and likeness, news of competing species more evolved/advanced than our own would obliterate humanity's (and religions') exclusive relationship with the Divine.

Yet it is this Divine relationship in each one of us that shines through on a personal level, and transcends ethno-social and politico-religious differences. Once again we are for the most part aware, at least on the subconscious level that something much greater than us exists and that we are somehow absolutely intertwined with it. This might explain why fewer of us go to church, but more of us consider spirituality very important in our lives.

We possess an insatiable hunger to discover our supernatural nature and have an unquenchable thirst for knowledge about our link to the everlasting. The truly enlightened ones among us are busy at work ready to unlock any door to this knowledge that can be found, with science and the arts both converging on this same target. Perhaps at no time in human history have more people sought this knowledge across so many various fields of endeavor. Mankind is knocking on the Cosmic portal with a battering ram.

True, some say "Don't go through that door," afraid to disrupt the status quo. Some even refuse to admit the existence of the door, let alone what is behind it. But the genie is out of the bottle, and humanity has tasted the fruit from the tree of knowledge. There is no turning back, even if it helps once in a while to look back in order to remember and build on the knowledge already gained (and lost) over the eons. In our rush to find the answers to our questions of today, it would be foolish to forget the lessons of the past. After all, *hubris* was the one unforgivable sin in ancient Greece. To be guilty of it allowed no room for divergent opinion by others, and placed the smug perpetrator at the self-proclaimed pinnacle of wisdom (and in peril of his life).

"Blessed are those with eyes to see and ears to.hear", but "more blessed still to believe and not to have seen." Some things do come down to faith, and much about life is still (thankfully) a mystery. It wouldn't be much fun if we knew everything now, would it? But if we do know something is real, something we've experienced yet can't explain, or prove scientifically, the rest of us skeptics still need to recognize that mysterious things can still be real.

Living as we do in this modern age which could be called a technocracy, one part of us wants to believe only in "proven reality." But reality might be many (possibly contradictory) levels of existence. If you believe that we possess a soul, then we are spirits trapped in the material world. If you believe that there are dimensions of existence beyond this space/time continuum, then is this the real reality, or are we trapped in an illusionary construct? Science is start-

ing to bump into questions about life that sound suspicious-
ly like they belong in the realm of the philosophers and theo-
logians, who in turn are finding surprising solace in scientific discovery, narrowing what used to be an unbridgeable
chasm between these competing worlds of thought. While
we do exist in this time and space we call reality, occasional
tantalizing glimpses beyond the boundaries happen every
day. Dreams, intuition, pre-cognition, prayer, meditation -
even various art forms - transcend this existence and point
toward a different "reality." Sadly, so does the epidemic
use of mind altering drugs, (and an alarming suicide rate)
especially among teenagers. There seems to be a natural
longing to leave this existence, if only for a while, through
movies, books, music, or travel, all of which temporarily
engage our imagination and transport us to an alternate
reality on a daily basis.

You can now use another way to consciously explore
this human duality of incarnate spirit. It's demonstratably
real in this reality and brings us to an alternate awareness
of ourselves and others. Everyone has it. Anyone can see
it. Science can measure it, even photograph it. Mystics have
talked about it for centuries. Artists have depicted it, healers have used it, and we have all felt it: The aura is a very
special physical manifestation of our human duality.

Can we change the world with this knowledge of how
to see the aura?

No, at least not immediately.

Will it bring a better understanding of who we are
and what we are all about?

You bet it will!

As individuals, we also have within our grasp the
ability to control our health and well being on a day-to-day
basis. Learning about the aura is one way to gauge and

monitor our health on an entirely different scale and this knowledge can be used to augment our growing awareness of the effects that various aspects of our environment have on us. With luck we might also be able to say that in the next five or ten years 80% of our total knowledge of self will have been gained. The capability is there, we must learn about and then use this knowledge. Don't let fear or the "naysayers" hold you back.

Our conditioning against the belief in "otherworldly" or "extra-sensory" events is very strong. Auras are just one more thing we've been conditioned to believe couldn't possibly exist. That certainly was my first reaction when I was taught to see them. But as I became comfortable and adept at seeing the aura I began to realize how natural and "this-worldly" our visible magnetic/electric field had become. Piece by piece, my resistance and skepticism have been crumbling ever since.

As you become more adept at seeing the energy field around yourself and others, you might become curious, as I did, in other related fields of study. If you already have interests in these areas, auric perception will (hopefully) augment your knowledge. Too often we look for answers everywhere but where real knowledge resides: within the self. Auric vision, once attained, is but one threshold crossed in a return journey to further self knowledge and fulfillment...

# XV

## Auric Exercises

### To See An Individual's Aura

1.  Stand the subject 18" to 2' in front of a bare white wall. Avoid colors or patterns on the wall.

2.  Use indirect lighting, natural ambient daylight if possible. Avoid fluorescent or direct sunlight.

3.  View the subject from at least ten feet away.

4.  Ask the subject to relax, breathe deeply and to rock gently from side-to-side, with hands unclasped at his or her sides.

5.  Look past the subject's head and shoulders and focus on the wall behind them.

6.   Avoid looking at the person by concentrating on the texture of the paint or whatever surface is behind the subject.

7.   As you look past the outline of the  body,  where the air starts and the body stops you will see a band of fuzzy light around the subject, about one-quarter to one-half inch in depth.  This is the etheric aura.

8.   Continue to look past the outline of the body and you should see the subject as if he is illuminated from behind, sometimes with a bright yellow or silver color.  One side might glow more  brightly or slowly pulsate.  Auras are rarely uniform.

9.   Each person is different.  Some subjects will have less visible auras than others and colors will not always be seen at first by every viewer.  The fuzzy envelope or "halo" around the body will be decernable within a very short time,  usually within one minute or less.

10.  Try using different subjects and experiment with lighting and background.  Soon you will see a second, larger band of light  3" to 2' around the body. This is the astral aura and it is usually darker and more diffuse.

## To See Your Own Aura

1. Stand in front of a mirror at least 18" away, further if possible.

2. Place yourself with a white or neutral color surface visible in the mirror behind you, again 18" or more is ideal.

3. Relax, breathe deeply and sway gently from side to side.

4. Focus on the texture of the surface of the wall behind you.

5. As you stare past the outline of your head and shoulders you will see the envelope of light around your body move with you as you rock gently.

6. Remember to breathe as you do this, since you are now both viewer and subject.

7. Lighting should be subdued, neither too bright, nor too dark. Experiment. Auras can not be seen in total darkness, and bright light will wash out all but the most vibrant of auras.

8.      Color of clothing is unimportant. You might find that your auric color, when you become accustomed to seeing it, will clash with certain items in your wardrobe, but you will see your true colors regardless of what you wear.

9.      Experiment with projecting a color. Think of a color and try to visualize it. You can change your baseline color temporarily through this kind of exercise, and the change can be seen.

10.     As you exhale, notice that the aura should get larger. Reciting the numbers 1 through 30 in a normal speaking voice will help liberate your energy. Take a breath after every two numbers. Speed up the count from the number 20 on without taking a breath and watch your aura shrink in size and vibrancy. As you resume normal quiet breathing, the aura will return to its former size, but might appear a little brighter.

# COLOR CHART

RED       *Physical life, vitality, ambition, sexual power. Dark or cloudy red shows violent or passionate tendencies. "Red with rage." Centered on the genital area. The root chakra.*

ORANGE    *Energy and health, physical vitality, dynamic force. Pride can result from an excess in the aura, dark or cloudy orange shows low intellect. Centered in the stomach/spleen area.*

YELLOW    *Love and kindness, compassion, optimism. Dark, lifeless yellow shows suspicion, covetousness. Centered in the solar plexus/ heart region. "Breath of life."*

GREEN    *Balance, harmony, healing, the calming force. Clear green shows adaptability, versatility. Dark shades are deceitful, jealous. "Green with envy." Located in the thyroid/neck area.*

BLUE    *Strong mental powers, intelligence, logical thinking. Clear "out of the" blue shows intuitive capabilities. Dark shades show over-analytic suspicious nature or "visionary" mentality. Centered in the brain.*

VIOLET    *Inspired thought, or deep wisdom. Can show spirituality and devotional nature. Artistic and harmonious with nature. Self mastery. Located in pineal gland.*

PURPLE    *Symbol of spiritual attainment, divine connection, mystical understanding, cosmic consciousness. Located in the pituitary gland. "Purple rainment." The crown chakra.*

# *OTHER COLORS*

SCARLET    *Lust, lower passions, materialism.*

ROSE PINK    *Selfless love. Gentleness, modesty.*

BROWN    *Avarice, selfishness.*

GOLD    *Higher self, good qualities, harmonious.*

SILVER    *Versatility, high energy, constant change.*

GREY    *Depression, low energy, fear.*

BLACK    *Sinister, malicious, evil intent.*

# *Colors Relating to Chakras of the Body*

VIOLET
*(Spirit)*

BLUE
*(Mind)*

GREEN
*(Thyroid)*

YELLOW
*(Heart)*

ORANGE
*(Spleen)*

RED
*(Genital)*

# Coming Soon...

### *Let's Feel How We See*

Mark Smith's next book will develop and enhance your ability to not only see the aura, but *feel* the aura.

Available March 1996